Contents

Introduction

A colourful past and age-old traditions combine with an abundance of scenic beauty and 21st-century modernity to make Lithuania a fascinating and rewarding destination for travellers of any persuasion. For a relatively small country, Lithuania packs in a huge variety of experiences, offering everything from perfectly preserved medieval towns steeped in history and magnificent national parks to cutting-edge modern facilities. Plunging from sweltering summers into the coldest and snowiest of winters, visiting Lithuania is a rewarding experience at any time of year.

Urbanites will enjoy Lithuania's three largest and very different cities. The capital Vilnius, the inter-war capital Kaunas, and the old German port of Memel, now Lithuania's third city, Klaipėda, are all fascinating destinations. Wandering around their streets is like a lesson in the development of European architecture, with examples from as early as the 13th century, through the Gothic, Baroque and Renaissance eras, to the ultra-modern. Museums and galleries are everywhere, particularly in Vilnius, which has enough to keep you busy for a day or two. Evening entertainment ranges from the sophisticated to folksy traditions in music.

Travellers who consider retail therapy an essential part of a holiday won't be disappointed by the shopping options either. All the major destinations listed in this guidebook have excellent shops, providing opportunities to pick up bargains in a range of outlets from international fashion chains to traditional gift shops and classic Soviet-style markets. Local specialities such as amber and high-quality craft items are widely available.

If relaxation is what you need, there are plenty of places to choose from. Sun, sea and sand (of which only the latter two can be guaranteed) can be found in abundance along Lithuania's Baltic coast. The extraordinary natural phenomenon of the Curonian Spit, now the Neringa National Park, encapsulates sand dunes, beaches and pristine pine forests brimming with wildlife.

Just north of Klaipėda, situated on this stretch of coast, are a multitude of small resorts, among them the country's summer capital Palanga, Lithuania's premier seaside resort and favourite hedonists' destination. Here you can enjoy dunes and sandy beaches side by side with the beautiful

Botanical Park. Palanga is a busy, thriving town with all the attractions of a highly popular seaside resort. It's also known as a health resort, with several hotels offering specialised treatments. However, if it's the ultimate spa holiday you're looking for, Druskininkai, in the south of the country, is the place for you. One of the earliest spa centres in Europe, Druskininkai has a wonderful microclimate, scenic beauty and all the treatments you could possibly want.

There are plenty of places to enjoy Lithuania's fabulous natural wealth of lakes and forests, its landscapes of gentle hills and fertile plains. The country boasts five national parks and numerous regional ones. Aside from spearheading conservation efforts, these offer a range of activities from walks to boating and bird watching.

In terms of simple practicalities, Lithuania's transport infrastructure is excellent. Routes are well signposted, and getting from one place to another is pretty much hassle-free. And, once the ice is broken, the Lithuanians are a friendly, hospitable people who are speaking more and more English as the years progress. Their love of the country is readily apparent, and they're proud to help you enjoy the best of it.

Kaunas Old Town

Land and people

Six centuries ago, during Lithuania's pagan days, the forests were considered sacred and worshipped. Today, the people of Lithuania still treasure their woodlands. The Pateriai-born poet Sigitas Geda (1943–) reflected this national passion when he wrote that 'a person who doesn't understand the earth, ocean and the trees is a barbarian'. The Lithuanians still like to name their children after the country's former Grand Dukes and aspects of its nature, and it's this direct link to the past that makes Lithuania such an interesting cultural experience.

Flanked by the Baltic Sea to the west, Lithuania shares its borders with four countries, namely Latvia, Belarus, Poland and the Russian *oblast* (province) of Kaliningrad. The country is located right in the middle of Europe; in fact, a spot 26km (16 miles) north of Vilnius was designated as the centre of Europe by the French National Geographical Institute in 1989. Covering over 65,300sq km (25,200sq miles), Lithuania is approximately the same size as Ireland. It's also both the largest, and, with around three and a half million inhabitants, the most densely populated of the three Baltic States.

With over 90km (56 miles) of sand along the Baltic coast and a predominance of gentle rolling plains and extensive forests, the country's landscape is diverse. Amounting to 55 per cent of the total land area, the plains comprise three lowland regions, the Pajuris Lowland, the Middle Lowland and the Eastern Lowland, and three upland plateaux, the Žemaičiai (or Baltic) Upland, the Aukštaičiai Upland and the Eastern Upland. At 293.6m (964ft), Juozapinė Hill, southeast of Vilnius on the Belarusian border, is the highest point in Lithuania. The soil of the Middle Lowland plains, especially near the rivers, is the most fertile.

Woodlands today constitute only about 28 per cent of the total land area of this once heavily forested country. The dominant species are pine, spruce and birch. The once abundant ash and oak groves are now scarce. The forests are rich in mushrooms and berries too, providing a popular annual free source of food for many.

The country boasts a fairly large network of waterways. Nearly 3,000 lakes cover over 880sq km (340sq miles). The biggest concentration of

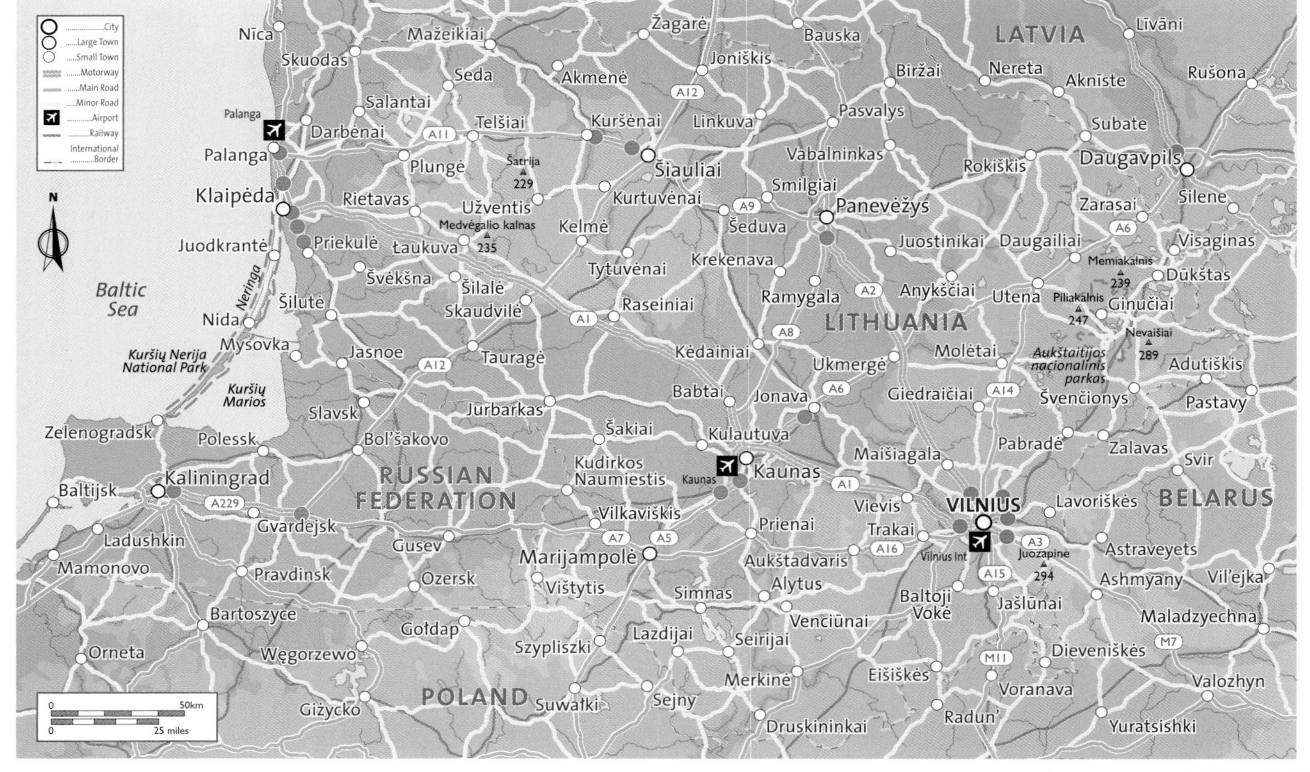
City
Large Town
Small Town
Motorway
Main Road
Minor Road
Airport
Railway
International Border
N
0 50km
0 25 miles
LATVIA
LITHUANIA
BELARUS
RUSSIAN FEDERATION
POLAND
Baltic Sea
Kuršių Nerija National Park
Kuršių Marios
Neringa
Aukštaitijos nacionalinis parkas
Nīca
Mažeikiai
Žagarė
Bauska
Līvāni
Skuodas
Seda
Akmenė
Joniškis
Biržai
Nereta
Aknīste
Rušona
Salantai
Telšiai
Kuršėnai
Linkuva
Pasvalys
Subate
Palanga
Darbėnai
Plungė
Šatrija 229
Šiauliai
Vabalninkas
Rokiškis
Daugavpils
Klaipėda
Rietavas
Užventis
Kurtuvėnai
Smilgiai
Panevėžys
Zarasai
Silene
Medvėgalio kalnas 235
Kelmė
Šeduva
Juodkrantė
Priekulė
Laukuva
Tytuvėnai
Krekenava
Juostinikai
Daugailiai
Visaginas
Memiakalnis 239
Dūkštas
Švėkšna
Šilalė
Raseiniai
Ramygala
Anykščiai
Utena
Piliakalnis 247
Ginučiai
Šilutė
Skaudvilė
Nida
Nevaišiai 289
Mysovka
Jasnoe
Tauragė
Kėdainiai
Ukmergė
Molėtai
Adutiškis
Babtai
Jonava
Giedraičiai
Švenčionys
Pastavy
Slavsk
Jurbarkas
Šakiai
Kulautuva
Pabradė
Zalavas
Zelenogradsk
Polessk
Bol'šakovo
Maišiagala
Svir
Kudirkos Naumiestis
Kaunas
Kaliningrad
Baltijsk
Vievis
VILNIUS
Lavoriškės
Gvardejsk
Vilkaviškis
Prienai
Trakai
Ladushkin
Gusev
Marijampolė
Aukštadvaris
Vilnius Int
Juozapinė 294
Astraveyets
Mamonovo
Pravdinsk
Ozersk
Vištytis
Simnas
Alytus
Baltoji Vokė
Ashmyany
Vil'ejka
Bartoszyce
Gołdap
Lazdijai
Venciūnai
Jašlūnai
Maladzyechna
Orneta
Węgorzewo
Szypliszki
Seirijai
Dieveniškės
Merkinė
Eišiškės
Voranava
Valozhyn
Giżycko
Suwałki
Sejny
Druskininkai
Radun'
Yuratsishki
A11
A12
A9
A1
A2
A8
A6
A14
A229
A7
A5
A16
A3
A15
M11
M7

Evening shadows in a Klaipėda street

bodies of water is in the eastern part of the country, although the largest inland body of water, the Kuršių Marios (Curonian Lagoon), is in the west, separating the Kuršių Nerija (Curonian Spit) from the mainland and the Baltic Sea.

Lithuania's five national parks, established over the last 30 years, protect forested land in the southern part of the country, the lakes in the northeast and the seaboard in the west. All the parks include wonderful museums showcasing exhibits and collections of local cultural heritage, and are outstanding places for recreation and relaxation. Accommodation can be found in a range of traditional village houses and hostels as well as the occasional hotel.

Ethnographic regions

Lithuania is broadly divided into four main regions, which are ethnographically and ecologically distinct. Aukštaitija, Dzūkija, Suvalkija and Žemaitija differ from each other in their character, dialects and folk traditions, as well as their flora and fauna.

The largest region, Aukštaitija covers the middle, east and north of the country. The name is derived from the word *aukštas* (high), after the hilly uplands in this region. Aukštaitija is extremely popular with local tourists during the summer because of its fine forests and beautiful lakes. The area has the greatest number of lakes, with the country's largest, Drūkšiai, and deepest, Tauragnas, both located here. The forests are some of the oldest in the country and lay claim to the oldest tree, the 1,500-year-old oak tree in the tiny village of Stelmužė.

In the settled countryside, farms tend to be divided into smaller holdings. Many in this area have been designated ethnographic farms, where the attempt is to maintain a traditional way of life. There are plenty of tourist information centres and museums too, including the Beekeeping Museum in Stripeikiai (*see p124*). For the beer enthusiast, two of Lithuania's largest breweries in Utena (Utenos) and Panevėžys (Kalnapilis) are also in this region.

Suvalkija, in the southwest, is the smallest region and is named after the town of Suvalkai, now called Suwałki, just over the border in Poland. The proximity to Poland may have a bearing on the region's culinary speciality *skilandis*, which is a kind of smoked sausage filled with savoury minced meat. The region is mainly agricultural, with smallholdings characterised by farmsteads surrounded by trees.

Dzūkija, the southern region of Lithuania, borders Poland and Belarus. Flanking the Nemunas River, most of it is under forest cover. A major feature of the region therefore relates to woodland culture. Large wooden carvings can be seen dotted along many roads and in the forests themselves. Botanical reserves and ancient villages connected to the life of the forest reinforce this culture. As every autumn approaches, mushrooms on the forest floors draw mushroom pickers (*grybautojai*) from far afield. The region's main town is the famous old health spa of Druskininkai, which attracts many Lithuanians and an increasing number of foreign tourists.

The Basilian Gate in Vilnius

Recorded as Samogitia as early as the 13th century, Žemaitija is the westernmost region of the country. The locals are an industrious lot, but not noted for a propensity to change. The Žemaitija National Park is very popular in summer, but the region's claim to fame is as the country's dairy centre. An interesting peculiarity of the region is the *Žemaitukas* horse. In danger of extinction until recently, this short, strong and energetic beast is happily beginning to increase in numbers.

Climate

A maritime climate prevails in the 12–15km (7½–9½-mile) wide coastal zone in the west, while towards the eastern part it becomes continental. The country is characterised by four seasons, with moderate heat in summer. Summers are also marked by normal humidity as well as an adequate number of sunny days. Winters, however, are long, with temperatures sometimes plummeting to as low as –30°C (–22°F), and the period of vegetative growth short (just 169–202 days). July is the warmest time of the year, with temperatures rising to 20°C (68°F) and higher. But don't get too excited, for July is also the wettest month of the year.

Ethnic groups

Over 80 per cent of the country's population is ethnic Lithuanian.

Typical Lithuanian woodcarvings

However, there are also people of an unbelievable 115 different ethnic backgrounds scattered throughout the country. The second largest ethnic group is the Poles (6.74 per cent) who, unsurprisingly, mainly live in the southeast of the country. Other large groups are Russians (6.31 per cent), Belarusians (1.23 per cent) and Ukrainians (0.65 per cent). Unlike in neighbouring Latvia and Estonia, there are no serious ethnic tensions in Lithuania.

Possibly as a result of the Lithuanian experience of occupation and oppression over the centuries, there is great respect shown to ethnic minorities. The Constitution of the Republic of Lithuania guarantees ethnic minorities the right to cultivate their own languages, traditions and cultures. The 1989 Law on Ethnic Minorities, amended in 1991, guarantees all citizens of the Republic of Lithuania equal political, social and economic rights. A special government department dedicated to the needs of minority communities also looks after the needs of Lithuanians living abroad, and is the first of its kind in Eastern and Central Europe.

Bilingual education is promoted, and Lithuanian radio and television stations broadcast in a number of different languages. Publication of periodicals and newspapers in languages other than Lithuanian is encouraged, as are the establishment and membership of public organisations for ethnic minorities.

Such respect for diversity has by no means meant a diminution of indigenous culture and beliefs. The high percentage of ethnic Lithuanians has made it relatively easy for them to nurture and preserve their culture, and their traditions remain as strong as ever.

Religion

Before the acceptance of Christianity in 1387, pagan religious practices were the norm for Lithuanians and remained popular in folk culture for several hundred years afterwards.

In contemporary Lithuanian society, the dominant religion is Roman Catholicism, professed by most Lithuanians and the ethnic Poles. According to population census data, over 70 per cent of all residents subscribe to the Catholic Church.

Roman Catholicism appeared in the Grand Duchy of Lithuania in the 14th century, around the same time as the emergence of Karaite, Jewish and Tartar religious traditions in the country. Protestants made an appearance in the 16th century and were joined by Old Believers in the 17th century. The majority of citizens of Russian origin belong to the Russian Orthodox Church.

The Constitution doesn't make provision for a state religion but specifically protects the freedom of thought, conscience and religion of all Lithuanian citizens. The state recognises traditional Lithuanian churches and religious organisations as well as other denominations and religious organisations, provided that they show a commitment to Lithuanian society, and that their teachings and rituals contradict neither morality nor the law.

GEOGRAPHICAL DATA

Population
Lithuania 3,385,000
Vilnius 580,000
Kaunas 362,000
Klaipėda 186,500

Longest rivers
Nemunas 937km/582 miles (359km/223 miles in Lithuania)
Neris 510km/317 miles (235km/146 miles in Lithuania)
Venta 350km/218 miles (167km/104 miles in Lithuania)

Largest lakes
Drūkšiai 4,480ha/11,070 acres (3,480ha/8,600 acres in Lithuania)
Dysnai 2,439ha/6,030 acres
Dusia 2,334ha/5,770acres

Highest hills
Juozapinė 294m/965ft
Nevaišiai 289m/948ft

The belfry next to the cathedral, Vilnius

The 1995 Law on Religious Societies and Communities confirmed nine religious groups as recognised by the state, namely Roman Catholics, Greek Catholics (Uniates), the Orthodox Church, Old Believers, Evangelical Reformers, Evangelical Lutherans, Jews, Karaite and Sunni Muslims. These communities have coexisted in Lithuania for over 300 years. The Law also includes provisions for the procedures that religious communities need to follow in order to obtain state recognition. The Seimas (Parliament) may award this recognition on the condition that the religious community has been formally registered and practising in the country for at least 25 years. The community also needs to have public support, and must be adequately integrated into Lithuanian society and cultural heritage.

History

600–100 BC The first Baltic tribes establish themselves on the territory that is now known as Lithuania.

1236 Duke Mindaugas defeats the Livonian Knights and unites local chieftains at the Battle of Saule, thus setting the stage for the founding of the state of Lithuania.

1253 Duke Mindaugas is crowned Lithuania's king on 6 July (now the Day of Lithuanian Statehood).

1323 The first mention of Vilnius in written text during the reign of Grand Duke Gediminas, who invites craftsmen and merchants to settle there.

1325 Gediminas forms an alliance with Poland by marrying his daughter to the Polish king's son.

1387 Lithuania converts to Christianity.

1390 Vilnius, its buildings mostly of timber, is burnt to the ground by the Teutonic Knights.

1392–1430 The reign of Vytautas the Great.

1410 The Battle of Žalgiris (Polish Grunwald) sees the joint Polish-Lithuanian armies defeat the Teutonic Order.

1500s The Renaissance heralds Lithuania's Golden Age.

1569 The so-called Lublin Union establishes a joint Polish-Lithuanian state.

1579 The founding of Vilnius University.

1795 Lithuania is annexed by Tsarist Russia. Vilnius is relegated to the status of a provincial town. Its defensive walls are destroyed.

1831 Amidst significant revolt against the Russian occupation, Vilnius University is shut down and Catholic churches closed and converted to Russian Orthodox use.

1834 The installation of an optical telegraph line,

	stretching from St Petersburg via Vilnius to Warsaw.
1861	Serfdom is abolished.
1863	Another revolt against the tsar fails and oppressive measures are increased.
1905	Russia is defeated by Japan, signalling the decline of the Tsarist empire.
1918	The Council of Lithuania proclaims the restoration of an independent Lithuanian state.
1920	Vilnius is incorporated within the Polish border. Kaunas becomes the Lithuanian capital.
1923	The former Prussian city of Memel is renamed Klaipėda and incorporated into Lithuania.
1939	The signing of the Molotov-Ribbentrop Pact divides Eastern Europe between Nazi Germany and the USSR, putting Lithuania under Soviet influence. Soviets restore Vilnius as the Lithuanian capital in return for the right to set up military bases in the region.
1940	The Soviet Union occupies and annexes Lithuania.
1941–4	Lithuania is occupied by Nazi Germany. Almost the entire Jewish population of the country dies in the Holocaust. The country is reincorporated into the Soviet Union.
1990	The Supreme Council of the Republic of Lithuania declares the restoration of independence.
1991	Lithuania joins the UN.
1994	Lithuania joins the NATO Partnership for Peace Programme. Signs treaty of friendship with Poland.
2003	Rolandas Paksas wins the presidential elections. Lithuanian voters say yes to EU accession.
2004	Lithuania becomes a member of both the EU and NATO. Paksas is found guilty of underhand dealings and Valdas Adamkus is voted into power.
2009	Vilnius designated a European captial of culture.

From occupation to independence

Lithuania's difficult fate through the 20th century can be in part attributed to the 1939 Molotov-Ribbentrop Pact, an agreement on how the then independent countries of Eastern Europe would be divided between the two totalitarian regimes of Nazi Germany and the Soviet Union. The countries included in the pact were Finland, Estonia, Latvia, Lithuania, Poland and Romania. Soviet control was to cover the first four. Poland was to be partitioned between the two signatories. All these countries were invaded by either the Soviets or Nazi Germany, or both, at some point during World War II.

Once the partition of Poland was complete, the Soviets wasted no time in exerting huge pressure on the countries in their sphere of influence. They persevered until all the states, except Finland, had signed pacts of 'defence and mutual assistance', which allowed the USSR to set up Soviet bases in their countries. Lithuania was invaded and annexed by the USSR in 1940, and then

Grim reminders of Lithuania's constant struggle against invading powers

occupied by the Third Reich from 1941 to 1944, when it was retaken by the Soviets. These two occupations led to the almost total genocide of Lithuania's Jewish population under Hitler's Final Solution, and the deportation of tens of thousands of Lithuanians to Siberia under Stalin's reign of terror.

The Soviets imposed a totalitarian system on Lithuania, including a planned economy, one-party rule, surveillance and terror carried out by the NKVD and later the KGB. At the end of World War II, resistance against the Soviets remained pretty strong in Lithuania, with Lithuanian partisans, the so-called Forest Brothers, fighting the occupation until the mid-1950s. The Khrushchev era, which followed the death of Stalin in 1953, brought about a slight liberalisation, and Lithuanians gradually began to make inroads into the Communist Party.

In 1988, the founding of the independent Sąjūdis movement marked a turning point in Lithuanian history. Sąjūdis, along with like-minded Estonian and Latvian groups, celebrated the 50th anniversary of the Molotov-Ribbentrop Pact in 1989 by organising the largest ever mass protest in the Baltics with over two million people linking hands in a human chain covering a distance of over 600km (370 miles) all the way from the Estonian capital Tallinn, via Latvia's capital Riga, and ending outside Vilnius Cathedral. Finally, in February 1990, after some 50 years of Soviet occupation, Sąjūdis won a sweeping majority of the seats in the local Supreme Council elections, and on 10 March 1990, Lithuania was able to proclaim its independence, the first of the Soviet-occupied states to do so. However, Moscow refused to accept this. Its attempts at resisting change and forced intervention led to 14 unarmed civilians being killed at the Vilnius Television Tower on 13 January 1991.

In 1991, Moscow finally recognised Lithuanian independence. Later that year, Lithuania attained international recognition when it was admitted to the United Nations on 17 September. The Lithuanian currency, the *litas*, was reintroduced in 1993. In February of the same year, Algirdas Brazauskas (1932–), Lithuania's last First Secretary of the Lithuanian Communist Party, became the first directly elected President of Lithuania.

Also in 1993, the last Russian troops left Lithuania. The country voted to join the EU in 2003 and was granted membership in May 2004. Later in the same year, it became a member of NATO, becoming an independent player on the global stage.

Politics

The Republic of Lithuania (Lietuvos Respublika) *is now a stable state governed by a system of parliamentary democracy. Formally known as the Lithuanian Soviet Socialist Republic, Lithuania declared independence from the Soviet Union in March 1990, although the Soviet Union didn't recognise Lithuania's independence until 6 September 1991. Like so many former communist countries, many of its contemporary democratic leaders' political origins can be traced back to the heady days of the Soviet state.*

The foundations of the country's political and social system are enforced by the Fundamental Law (the Constitution), which was adopted on 25 October 1992. The Constitution also sets out the rights, freedoms and obligations of its citizens. The powers of the state are shared between the Seimas (Parliament), the President, the Government and the Judiciary. The scope of the powers of each of these branches is defined by the Constitution.

The President's Palace in Vilnius

Seimas (Parliament)

The supreme body of state power in Lithuania is the Seimas. At present it comprises 141 deputies, who are elected for a four-year period. Of the 141 seats in the Seimas, 71 members are directly elected by popular vote, while the remaining 70 are elected by proportional representation. The Seimas has a wide range of powers, consisting of the following:

- The power to adapt and amend the Constitution.
- The power to adopt laws, to consider drafts on the programmes produced by the Government and to approve them.
- The power to control the activities of the Government, to approve the budget of the Government, and to establish the state institutions provided by the law.
- The power to appoint and dismiss chairpersons of the state institutions, and to settle other issues pertaining to state power.

President

The highest official of the state, the President of Lithuania is elected for a five-year term directly by Lithuanian citizens over the age of 18 on the basis of universal, equal and direct suffrage by secret ballot.

The President plays a key role through the following functions:

- To consider the major political problems of foreign and domestic affairs.
- To appoint and dismiss state officials as provided by the Constitution and other laws.
- To proclaim a state of emergency if required.
- To approve and publish the laws adopted by the Seimas or return them with remarks for reconsideration.

LITHUANIA ON THE INTERNATIONAL STAGE

The Republic of Lithuania is a member of many international organisations, the most significant of these being the European Union, the United Nations, NATO and the World Trade Organisation.

FURTHER READING

Before he retired, Alfred Erich Senn was a professor emeritus of history at the University of Wisconsin who specialised in Eastern Europe and spent several years in the 1970s and 1980s trying to get permission from Moscow to visit Lithuania. After many failed attempts, Senn was finally given a visa, the timing of which happened to coincide with the beginning of the end of the Soviet Union and the parallel rise of the Lithuanian nationalist, pro-independence Sąjūdis movement in 1988. The professor's time spent among the leaders of Sąjūdis and witnessing all of the major events that led to Lithuania's 1990 independence became the subject of a superb book, *Lithuania Awakening* (University of California Press, 1990). Essential reading for anyone with even a passing interest in the collapse of the Soviet Union, the book is becoming increasingly hard to obtain. If you can't find it in a Lithuanian bookshop, its contents can be found for free online at the rather awkward address *http://ark.cdlib.org/ark:/13030/ft3x0nb2m8*

A ceremonial soldier guarding the Signatory House

HUMAN RIGHTS

All Lithuanian citizens have the right to participate in the Government, both directly and through their freely elected representatives. They have the right of equal opportunity to serve in a state office. Every citizen is guaranteed the right to criticise the work of state institutions and their officers, and to appeal against their decisions. It is prohibited to persecute citizens for expressing this criticism. Citizens are also guaranteed the right to petition.

- To perform other duties as specified in the Constitution.

On 27 June 2004, Valdas Adamkus was elected President of the Republic of Lithuania. The next election is scheduled for June 2009.

Government

The Lithuanian Government comprises the Prime Minister and Ministers. The Prime Minister is appointed or dismissed by the President, with the approval of the Seimas. Ministers are also appointed and dismissed by the President, based on the recommendation of the Prime Minister.

Within the limits of its competence, the Government's duties are as follows:

- To control the affairs of the country.
- To guard the inviolability of the territory, that is, the Republic.
- To ensure state and civilian security.
- To carry out resolutions of the Seimas on the enforcement of laws and the decrees of the President.
- To enter into and maintain diplomatic relations with foreign countries and international organisations.
- To perform the duties specified in the Constitution and other laws.

Judiciary

The Lithuanian legal system is based on the civil law system, in which all legislative acts can be appealed to the courts. This judicial system was established by Article 9 of the Constitution and by the Law on Courts passed in 1994. The judiciary has three branches, namely the Constitutional Court, the Supreme Court and the Court of Appeal. The judges for all courts are appointed by the President.

ADMINISTRATIVE DIVISIONS

Lithuania is divided into ten administrative divisions, namely Alytus, Kaunas, Klaipėda, Marijampolė, Panevėžys, Šiauliai, Tauragė, Telšiai, Utena and Vilnius. Each administrative unit is entitled to the right of self-government, which is implemented through Local Government Councils. Lithuanian citizens and other permanent residents of an administrative unit can be elected according to the law to Local Government Councils for a four-year term on the basis of universal, equal and direct suffrage. Voting is by secret ballot by the citizens of Lithuania and other residents of that administrative unit. The procedure for the organisation and activities of self-government institutions is established by law. Local Government Councils form executive bodies, which are accountable to the Councils for the direct implementation of the laws of the Republic of Lithuania and the decisions of the Government and the Local Government Council (Constitution of the Republic of Lithuania, Article 119).

Culture

As a nation, the Lithuanians are extremely proud of their history, culture and traditions. Through the many years of first Tsarist and then Soviet occupation, Lithuania succeeded in holding on to its culture and character, its art, music, song and dance. Today, classical music traditions thrive side by side with vibrant folk ones as well as all manner of contemporary art forms. These elements of culture combine to provide a truly enriching experience for visitors.

Folk music

Much Lithuanian folklore is based upon a rural outlook on life, with songs forming an integral and popular part of folk tradition. Folk music is at the heart of Lithuanian cultural heritage. Lithuanian folk songs are divided into categories such as family songs, historical and war songs, songs of protest, songs of Lithuanian emigrants, lullabies, wedding songs and others. There are many work songs which used to accompany all kinds of field and household chores, among them haymaking, harvesting, processing of flax, grinding grain, spinning and weaving.

War and historical songs tend to be less specific, not necessarily mentioning concrete historical

Detail of a Soviet-era bas-relief sculpture in Kaunas

A demonstration of traditional dancing

facts or indicating particular towns, villages or rivers. They usually feature images of seeing off a soldier to war and the period of waiting for his return.

Folk choreography

The Lithuanians have always loved to dance. Young people in the countryside still gather in the fields to dance during the summer, and indoors during the winter. Older people and children also take part in these festivities, talking, socialising and generally amusing themselves. Dance is central to Lithuanian folk traditions. Lithuanian folk choreography often takes the form of polyphonic singing dances, ring or circle dances or games.

These creative dances involve artistic imagery produced by rhythmical movements to vocal or instrumental music. Every movement and step in the dance has a purpose. Even a slight change of movement can symbolise a change in mood. As with Spanish flamenco although in an entirely different style, by creating a dance, Lithuanians simultaneously create a story.

The distinctiveness of Lithuanian folk choreography is also displayed in the accompanying music. The rhythm is calm and balanced, and the tempo is moderate. It's also purely lyrical, and tends to be narrative.

The first reference to Baltic folk dancing was at the end of the 9th century, by the traveller Vulfstan. Other travellers' accounts also mention how the Prussians and Lithuanians played and danced. Until the 20th century, dances were only occasionally documented and therefore only fragments of some dance descriptions remain. Often only the name of the dance and its mood were recorded; the music, steps or movements were not described.

From around the middle of the 20th century, two completely separate genres of folk dance movement have developed in Lithuania. The new type that has emerged is a stylised one, created by professional choreographers using music specially and professionally written. However, the genre of the traditional folk dance is still alive. Younger people learn these dances from their parents or grandparents, and the dances are also kept alive by folk groups, which still participate in folklore collection outings in rural areas.

Literature

Lithuania's literary tradition is considered to have begun with the publishing of Martynas Mažvydas' *Catechismus* in 1547. Lithuanian fiction didn't really feature as an art form until the 19th century, linking in with the general era of national reawakening. A famous early literary figure of the country was Kristijonas Donelaitis (1714–80). His poem *Metai* (The Seasons) was published in 1818, over half a century after it was written. Translated into many languages, it's now considered a national epic.

A statue representing a Lithuanian legend

The end of the 18th to the beginning of the 20th century was a difficult period for Lithuanian literature under Tsarist rule, and only a few exceptional poets emerged. Antanas Baranauskas and Maironis were two such, and they managed to elicit some protection from the secular authorities because of their status in the church.

Much of the great flowering of literature at the beginning of the 20th century can be seen as an attempt to rouse people to struggle for independence. Some of the great names of this period are Lithuania's most renowned female novelist Žemaitė, the master of the psychological novel Jonas Biliūnas, two patriotic writers Vincas Krėvė and Juozas Tumas-Vaižgantas, and the poet, prose writer and playwright Balys Sruoga. The memoirs of the latter, *Forest of the Gods*, about his experiences in a concentration camp, are one of the few works of that time published in English. A large number of Lithuania's finest writers of the 20th century fled the country during World War II, while some suffered grim periods of incarceration and torture, often ending in death.

Looking at Lithuanian literature as a whole, the period of the 1940s and 1950s was devastating, and it is only in the last few years that some of the country's émigré writers have been returning to Lithuania. A significant example is Czesław Miłosz (Lithuanian, Česlovas Milašus), who

Well-known romantic poet Adomas Mickevičius

won the Nobel Prize for Literature in 1980. Born near Kėdainiai in 1911, the Polish-speaking Miłosz lived outside the country from 1951, but was a frequent visitor before his death in Kraków in 2004 at the grand old age of 94. Poetry was his main domain, but one of his two novels, *The Issa Valley*, is set in rural Lithuania. He also wrote some political non-fiction works, of which *The Captive Mind* is worth reading. Those wishing to sample excerpts from current and classical Lithuanian literature should consult *Vilnius*, the magazine of the Lithuanian Writers' Union.

Art

From early times up to about the 13th and 14th centuries, art in Lithuania mainly consisted of decorative carving in wood. However, after the arrival of Christianity, Lithuanian fine arts tended to develop along religious lines. Portraits of senior clergy and the nobility became popular, as did illustrated manuscripts and biblical scenes. To appreciate the development of art in Lithuania up until the end of the 19th century, visit the Vilnius Picture Gallery (*see p49*) which has an excellent collection of paintings covering this period.

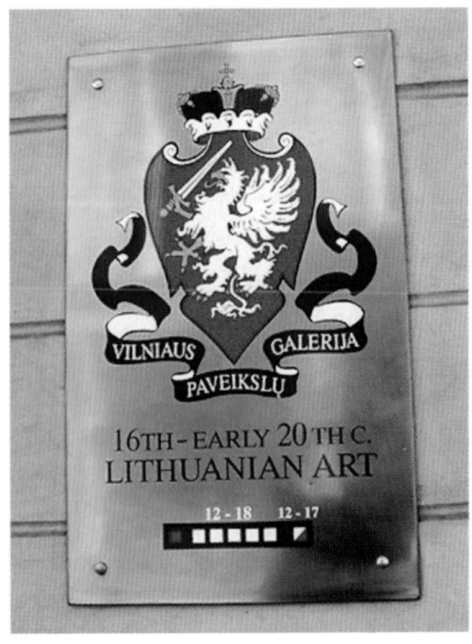

Vilnius Picture Gallery – spanning four centuries

The setting up of the Architecture Department at Vilnius University in 1793 marked the establishment of professional fine arts in Lithuania. It was led by the first exponent of Classicism, Laurynas Stuoka-Gucevičius. Pranciškus Smuglevičius was the first Professor of the Department of Drawing and Painting when it was set up in 1797. It was due to Smuglevičius' reputation that the Vilnius Arts School became a leading artistic centre in Lithuania and Poland. The department was later headed by the famous portrait painter Jonas Rustemas, whose teaching and inspiration in the early part of the 19th century had a huge influence on the development of Lithuanian painting.

Another landmark on the arts scene was the establishment of the Lithuanian Arts Society at the beginning of the 20th century. The first exhibition of serious Lithuanian art was organised by, among others, Lithuania's greatest creative genius Mikalojus Čiurlionis (*see p72*) in Vilnius in 1907. The combination of professional and folk art became a feature of the Lithuanian art scene, taking on a deep cultural importance. Another significant event during this time was the opening of the MK Čiurlionis Art Museum (*see p81*) in the then capital Kaunas in 1925.

The modern era in Lithuanian art dates from the mid-1950s and thrived under the relative liberalisation of the Krushchev regime. Graphic art in the 1950s and 1960s was mainly concerned with interpretations of folk art. Šiauliai-born Petras Repšys (1940–) is one of the country's outstanding figures in contemporary graphic art. His frescoes can be seen at Vilnius University and have come to be known as a significant expression of Baltic culture, incorporating historical, mythological and day-to-day aspects of tradition. The last decade of the 20th century has seen a huge change in artistic expression. Art institutions have changed dramatically, and state-owned and private galleries have appeared alongside each other.

Other traditions that are still very strong include various types of traditional handicrafts, and throughout the country you'll find numerous examples of handcrafted wood, amber and linen.

Theatre and music

The Tsarist regime banned Lithuanian theatre in the 19th century, but the Lithuanians kept it alive by running secret performances in barns or village houses. After 1904, when the Tsarist regime repealed its 40-year prohibition of the Latin alphabet, cultural societies sprang up all over the country. These societies encouraged the development of choirs, dance groups and drama societies, and helped to develop a national consciousness in theatre and other performances. The Soviet occupation was another stultifying time for Lithuanian theatre, but today it has no shortage of talented directors and is thriving once more.

World War II and the Soviet occupation also took their toll on the development of Lithuanian music. The multi-talented Mikalojus Čiurlionis is considered the founder of modern Lithuanian music and some of his compositions are typical of early 20th-century European music. A radical and innovative group of composers then emerged to challenge the musical scene, but the establishment of Soviet rule resulted in a return to the highly traditional, 19th-century Romantic style. This was to change in the 1980s when the new Romantics appeared, espousing the cause of the minimalist styles that are a feature of folk music. Perhaps the most famous and certainly the most radical musicians to come out of Lithuania during the Soviet period were the Russian-born Ganelin Trio, whose outrageous free jazz of the 1970s and 1980s flourished in Lithuania in a way that would never have been tolerated in Soviet Russia.

Detail of a sculpture in Kaunas

Festivals and events

Whether you are looking for traditional folk dancing, cutting-edge jazz or an international art show, Lithuania can provide everything you need. Vilnius hosts the majority of events, but this doesn't mean the rest of the country misses out. The website www.culture.lt *provides a good supply of up-to-date information in English. The year 2009 marks both the 1,000th anniversary of the Lithuanian state as well as Vilnius' status as one of the European capitals of culture. These two events will add heavily to an already-bursting cultural scene.*

January

Epiphany, Vilnius

The three Biblical kings walk the streets of the city, blessing children and giving them presents.

www.turizmas.vilnius.lt

Lake Sartai Horse Races

A series of extraordinary races on the frozen Lake Sartai near Utena, or next to it if it's a warm winter. The races begin in January, when the riders must qualify for the national finals held on the first Saturday in February.

www.zarasai.lt

February

Lithuanian Independence Day

A national holiday to mark Lithuania's independence, 16 February is celebrated in all parts of the country. Each area celebrates the restoration of the Lithuanian state in different ways.

www.lrkm.lt

Vilnius Book Fair

The biggest annual fair of its kind in the Baltics, attended by over 50,000 people. Organised by the Lithuanian Publishers' Association each February inside the Vilnius Litexpo centre.

www.litexpo.lt

March

Kaziukas Street Fair, Vilnius

Held over the first weekend of March, this is a traditional folk arts and crafts fair dedicated to the Patron Saint of Lithuania, St Casimir (Kaziukas). Events take place across the whole city.

www.turizmas.vilnius.lt

Spring Equinox

The Flag of Earth is hoisted and people plant trees to mark the Spring Equinox in Lithuania on 20–21 March.

www.lrkm.lt

April

International Jazz Festival, Kaunas

One of the most popular jazz festivals in Europe, featuring top international acts.

www.kaunasjazz.lt

International Dance Festival, Vilnius

One of the most outstanding festivals in the Baltics, this is a celebration of the New Baltic Dance.

www.turizmas.vilnius.lt

May

Skamba, Skamba Kankliai, Vilnius

A folklore festival held towards the end of the month and attracting performers from all over Lithuania and abroad. Concerts are held throughout the streets of the old town.

www.turizmas.vilnius.lt

June

Vilnius Festival

Since 1997, the Vilnius Festival has been held every summer. It starts in June and continues until July, featuring internationally renowned performers in the world of classical music. Both traditional and modern music are presented. Each year the festival embraces a different theme. The venues include the National Opera and Ballet Theatre, the Great Courtyard of Vilnius University and the Bernardine Church.

www.turizmas.vilnius.lt

Feast of St John's Night (Joninės)

This mystical event marks the summer solstice. Bonfires are lit, songs sung and pagan rituals revisited.

www.lrkm.lt

August

Visagino Country, Visaginas

Held in the entirely Soviet-built city of Visaginas close to the Latvian and Belarusian borders, this international country music event has got to be seen to be believed. The eccentric event of the year.

www.visaginocountry.lt

St Christopher Summer Music Festival, Vilnius

Festival of jazz, classical, organ and pop music.

www.turizmas.vilnius.lt

September

International Jazz Festival, Vilnius

Festival demonstrating Lithuania's prominent position in the world of jazz. It is the oldest annual event held in Vilnius.

www.vilniusjazz.lt

November

All Souls Day

Candles are lit at cemeteries across the country on the evening of 2 November.

www.lrkm.lt

December

Blukas

This holiday marks the shortest day of the year, 23 December. Old logs, symbolising evil spirits, are dragged down the streets and burnt. A nativity play is held in Vilnius.

www.lrkm.lt

The economy

One of the EU's fastest growing economies, the Lithuanian economy has greatly benefited from the country's mid-European geographical position. Its location facilitates trade with both Eastern and Western markets. However, since Lithuania conducts much more trade with Russia, more than the other two Baltic States, it was significantly affected by the 1998 Russian financial crisis, from which it has finally more or less recovered. Lithuania's gradual economic recovery has been facilitated by a combination of international and domestic factors, rising domestic consumption and growing investment introduced from abroad.

A local woman working in the fields in eastern Lithuania

Privatisation of the country's large and uneconomic state-owned utilities, particularly in the energy sector, is now nearing completion. Overall, more than 80 per cent of enterprises have been privatised to date. This is a giant leap towards a modern market economy from the central planning installed by the Soviet authorities.

Of the three Baltic States, Lithuania's economy is both the largest and overall the most diverse. The industrial sector, in particular, is extremely varied, and includes the production of chemicals, electronics, household appliances, pharmaceuticals, as well as wood and wood processing and the food industry. European Union membership since 2004 has encouraged many foreign companies to relocate to the country and manufacture at a more attractive price.

Trade is now increasingly oriented towards the Western market. Lithuania's membership of the World Trade Organisation has also aided its economic growth, and its strategic position is a draw for foreign investors who seek to attract business from the

Smart new restaurants are popping up all over

countries of the Baltic rim. Support from foreign governments and businesses has helped in the transition from the old command economy to a market economy.

However, the picture is not entirely rosy, with many Lithuanians still struggling to make ends meet. The picture is particularly bad in rural areas, where massive unemployment has led to a number of social problems ranging from increased theft to an alarming rise in alcohol consumption. Lithuania also remains the suicide capital of the world, with figures being almost three times the global average. Additionally, the increasing numbers of tourists to the country's larger cities have brought with them the inevitable beggars, a practice that the authorities are trying to outlaw.

The European Union and tourism

Lithuania was one of the ten new countries granted accession to the European Union in 2004. Membership of the EU has undoubtedly contributed to Lithuania's impressive economic growth in the last few years. As it surges forward economically, Lithuanians speak of a Baltic Tiger similar to the Celtic Tiger tag used to describe the Republic of Ireland. This economic development has undeniably been aided by membership of the European Union.

The country's tourist infrastructure, which has always been quite strong, has been expanding with additional EU funding. Roads are of a high quality, especially the main motorways. Indeed, of the three Baltic states, Lithuania definitely has the best roads. The tourist industry is becoming increasingly competitive. New businesses, hotels, resorts, restaurants, ATMs, petrol stations and supermarkets are appearing rapidly in towns and cities across the country. And the relatively competitive pricing is highly attractive for travellers from other European countries who have to contend with much higher prices at home for similar standards of service and facilities. It's no surprise, then, that Lithuania's tourism industry is booming.

Impressions

One of Lithuania's biggest assets is its excellent location. Positioned precisely at the centre of Europe, it is one of the main crossroads of the continent. The west–east connection between Paris, Berlin and Moscow is via Lithuania's capital Vilnius. The north–south line linking Helsinki with Athens also crosses the centre of Lithuania in Kaunas. Direct connections to most other European cities makes Vilnius, and hence Lithuania, an easily accessible destination.

When to go

Although summer is the most popular time to visit, the wide range of activities and sights makes Lithuania a delightful destination at any time of the year. This enthralling country offers places to see and things to do in them to suit all tastes and appetites for adventure all year round. Visiting Lithuania just before or after the peak season is a good idea. Although temperatures may be a little on the low side, if you do travel at these times, not only will you avoid the crowds but you'll also have the pick of the best restaurants and hotels. Booking in advance if you plan to visit during the summer is highly recommended.

Spring

Just before the summer months, around the end of April or start of May, the temperatures start to rise and the days become longer. This time of year is great for visiting the many national parks that Lithuania has to offer for a glimpse of nature at its best (*see pp128–39*). The cooler temperatures, as compared with those of summer, also make sightseeing in the cities more pleasurable.

Summer

The Baltic coast is the place to be in the summer, with Palanga (*see pp94–7*) being the most popular, albeit horribly loud and cramped, summer resort. Cool down after a spell of hot sun with a dip in the Baltic Sea. Another wonderful summer destination is the Curonian Spit, a long stretch of land between the Baltic Sea and the Curonian Lagoon. It offers unspoilt beaches, high dunes and scenic forest land. Lithuania's national parks and nature reserves are another must during the summer. You can simply relax by a lake, go boating or fishing, or indulge in a spa treatment.

Autumn

Early September marks the end of the peak tourist season. However, the weather can remain warm for a few weeks after this, and this period is known in Lithuania as *Bobų Vasara* (Grandma Summer). September is recommended for those travellers looking for more than relaxation on a beach. The cooler weather makes it more comfortable for sightseeing and active adventure. Furthermore, the streets of the old towns are less packed and the churches and museums less crowded. The national parks and nature reserves are beautiful in autumn as the leaves turn magnificent shades of yellow, red and orange and fall to carpet the ground. The downside of travelling at this time of year is that tourist services and facilities tend to get curtailed and service hours shortened. The weather is also less dependable.

Typical Lithuanian farmstead

The River Neris in winter

Winter

What better way to beat the winter blues than booking yourself into one of the spa treatment resorts here for a few days' pampering (*see pp74–5*)? Palanga is peaceful at this time of year, and is a lovely place to visit for a quiet rest with plenty of sea air. Many of its large number of spa hotels and sanatoriums stay open year round. In southern Lithuania, Druskininkai is the premier spa location. It's not a coastal resort, but it has the charm of a stately town surrounded by forests. Lithuania is significantly colder at this time of year, and you're more than likely to be surrounded by a frosty, snowy landscape. Depending on your mind-set and tolerance for the cold, this can be a bonus; the snow-covered vistas have a magical charm all their own. Lithuania offers limited skiing, although the flatness of the land in most areas is well suited to cross-country skiing rather than downhill runs. Another popular winter activity gaining popularity with tourists is ice-fishing. Most incoming tourism agencies now offer this as part of their winter itineraries.

Where to go

The three main cities make good weekend destinations at any time of year, with direct flights from several European cities now available (*see p174*). Vilnius, the capital and largest city in Lithuania, is in the southeast of the country, on the River Neris, and has much to offer. It has an old town packed with history and interesting buildings, and its new town offers as much as any other European city, with many high-street shopping chains, a bustling café culture and exclusive restaurants. Vilnius' nightlife doesn't go off peak either. The cities of Kaunas and Klaipėda are also busy year round.

The country's five main national parks, containing magnificent lakes and forests, are a must-see for all visitors. These are the Aukštaitija, Dzūkija, Kuršių Nerija, Trakai Historic and Žemaitija national parks. There are many other regional parks and nature reserves as well.

Offering a combination of city and beach life, the Baltic coast is one of Lithuania's main attractions. One of the coast's more pleasant experiences during the summer months is the contrast between the heat of the sun and the refreshing coolness of the sea.

Kaunas' oldest building, the castle, set at the meeting of the Neris and Nemunas rivers

What to wear

Layering is the key to comfort at all times of the year. July is the warmest (and wettest) month and January the coolest (*see p177*). In the summer it can get surprisingly hot, so light, breathable clothes are advisable when sightseeing. However, the evenings may get a bit cold even in summer, so always have a light jacket on hand. Bring a hat, gloves and scarf in winter, along with a heavy coat. Layers are particularly useful in winter. While it may be cold outside and you need to wrap up, if you stop at a café for a coffee, you'll be blasted with heat inside. The same goes for restaurants and bars. It may not be very cold in spring and autumn, but the winds can be chilly. It's advisable to bring a windcheater-style jacket if you're visiting at this time of year.

With an average annual rainfall of 66cm (26in) it will almost definitely rain at some point during your visit to Lithuania. A light rain jacket and umbrella are essential. In winter, sturdy waterproof walking shoes are recommended. Fur-lined ones are even better.

A discreet hideaway on the edge of the forest

Getting around

High-standard organised tours run from the main cities to the most popular nearby sights. Information on timings and destinations is available from local tourist offices and many hotels.

Riding on public transport in the main cities and towns isn't the most enjoyable experience Lithuania has to offer, especially during the busy rush hour periods in the three major cities. With the exception of small minibuses driving fixed routes that can be stopped anywhere in the street and a number of larger private buses, all public transport in Lithuania is state-owned. Tickets for the minibuses and private buses are always bought on board. Tickets for the state-owned transport can be bought from kiosks or directly from the driver for a slightly higher price. Prices for a single ticket (*bilietas*) range from around 1 to 3Lt depending on what you use.

More information about getting around the country can be found on p187.

Driving

Lithuanian roads were the pride and joy of the Soviets, and are still of a fairly high standard today. The main A1 highway running from Vilnius to

Klaipėda via Kaunas is excellent. Journey time for the 311km (193-mile) trip from the capital to the coast is around three and a half hours. Driving is on the right-hand side of the road. Traffic can be chaotic and occasionally idiotic, to put it mildly, so be careful if you decide to rent a car in Lithuania. While you may be a safe and experienced driver, the style and habits of Lithuanian drivers are somewhat less predictable. Seatbelts are compulsory under law, but you may not find many Lithuanians themselves wearing them. Lights must be on from 1 November to 1 March as well as during the first week in September. Drink-driving is not encouraged, and be aware that the blood-alcohol level limit is ridiculously low. Although improvements have been made, Lithuanian traffic police remain a sadly corrupt section of society.

Attitudes and etiquette

The Lithuanians are generally an outgoing and friendly people, but like many other Europeans can be a little cold when you first meet them. Lithuania is considered the most courageous of the Baltic states, as demonstrated by their resistance to Soviet oppression. They're also known for being more emotional than their Baltic neighbours. While being good-humoured and generally more talkative than the Latvians and the Estonians, they can also be more stubborn, and occasionally a little irritable when things don't go smoothly.

Most Lithuanians are pleased with the influx of tourists that has coincided with their EU membership. These hospitable folk will often go out of their way to try and help you. However, as a result of occasional

Tourists on Palanga beach

mutual language difficulties, you may not always receive what you requested!

There aren't too many formalities required of visitors. However, out of general respect for local traditions and mores, it's always better to ask if you're in doubt as to whether something is acceptable or not.

Nude sunbathing is generally not encouraged. There's a beach close to Nida on the Baltic Sea side that is designated naturist, but even that's divided into male and female zones. Alternatively, the coastal resort of Šventoji north of Palanga and close to the Latvian border has a mixed nudist beach.

Although no longer in the slightest bit essential, observing basic etiquette when visiting Catholic churches is always appreciated, especially by the older generation of Lithuanian worshippers. Men should keep their legs and, if possible, arms covered and remove their hats (the latter being the complete opposite when visiting a synagogue) when inside a church. Women should keep their shoulders covered if they can.

Language

The official language is Lithuanian, a fiendishly complicated lingo related to Latvian. Polish is spoken widely in Vilnius, German in Klaipėda. Russian is still understood throughout the country, even by many young people. English is becoming more and more

A typical roadside cross

popular, especially since EU accession in 2004, an event that began the mass exodus of Lithuanians to the UK and the Republic of Ireland. Although most people working in the tourist industry are expected to speak English, don't imagine that anyone working for the national railway company or long-distance bus companies speaks a word of it.

One of the oldest languages still spoken, Lithuanian allegedly dates back to the 5th century. It belongs to the family of Indo-European languages. Lithuanian is rich in dialects and regional accents and is spoken by some three million people in Lithuania, and by about one million people living in other countries such as Australia, Brazil, Belarus, Canada, Latvia, Poland, Russia and the USA.

Lithuanian is an entirely phonetic language, so if you learn what each letter sounds like, you'll be able to read it (without understanding a word of it, of course) straight away.

Suggested itineraries

Seven-day trip to Lithuania

Day 1 Arrive in Vilnius in the morning. After checking into your hotel, explore the old town (listed on the UNESCO heritage list). This is one of the most beautiful old cities in Eastern Europe. Stay the night at Vilnius.

Day 2 In the morning, see other important sights, such as the Church of St Peter and St Paul (*see p47*), or take the Circular walk (*see pp52–3*). In the afternoon, take a tour bus to Trakai.

Day 3 Leave in the morning for Kaunas via Druskininkai. From there, follow the drive to the Žuvintas Strict State Reserve (*see pp78–9*), continuing on to Kaunas in the afternoon. This is the second largest city in Lithuania and was the capital between the two World Wars. It also boasts a fabulous old town (*see pp86–7*). If you've got time, a trip to the Rumšiškės Open-air Museum (*see p60*) is recommended. Stay the night in Kaunas.

Day 4 Leave for Klaipėda in the morning. Spend the afternoon exploring the Curonian Spit.

Day 5 Travel north to the seaside resort of Palanga (*see pp94–7*). In the afternoon, either laze on the beach or if you're feeling like a trip in the car, drive to the Hill of Crosses (*see pp108–112*). Stay the night in Palanga.

Day 6 Drive back to Vilnius, enjoying the beautiful scenery on the way. In the evening, treat yourself to a farewell meal in one of the many fine restaurants Vilnius has to offer (*see pp166–7*). Stay the night in Vilnius.

Day 7 Depart in the morning for home.

BALTISH

Baltish is the clash of English with the Baltic languages, in which there are normally no survivors! Places to look out for Baltish are menus in restaurants, signs in hotel rooms, street signs converted directly from the local language into English and local tourist information translated into English.

Vilnius

When Lithuania regained its independence in 1990 after many centuries of occupation and destruction, Vilnius once again became the capital and centre of the nation. Since then it's been undergoing a huge programme of restoration and development, and is emerging as a multi-cultural European city of magnificent buildings and thriving enterprise. Lithuania celebrates its 1,000th anniversary in 2009, with its capital being chosen as one of the European Capitals of Culture for that year.

Vilnius has been the centre of political, commercial and cultural life in Lithuania since the city was founded by Grand Duke Gediminas in the 14th century (*see p12*). However, the city has been inhabited in one way or another since 2500–2000 BC, long before its formal founding. Vilnius' fortunes have always faithfully mirrored the country's through both thick and thin. Throughout Lithuania's fractured and turbulent history, including the Lithuanian-Polish Commonwealth that spanned the 17th and 18th centuries, annexation by Russia and Poland at various times, and occupation by Germany, Poland and Russia, Vilnius was one of the cities to bear the brunt of the downswings. And when Lithuania finally attained its independence and the economic, cultural and social revival of the country began, Vilnius was the first to benefit.

Universiteto Street in the Old Town

The city stands at the confluence of the Neris and Vilnia rivers, with hills rising from the riverbanks. Gediminas Hill, at 48m (157ft), is the highest of these and is the seat of Vilnius' great landmark, the Higher Castle. Pleasantly compact, most of the major sights in the capital can be seen on foot.

The city's tourist information website can be found at

www.turizmas.vilnius.lt. Vilnius has three tourist information centres:
Didžioji 31. Tel: (8-5) 262 64 70.
Geležinkelio 16 (Train Station). Tel: (8-5) 269 20 91.
Vilniaus 22. Tel: (8-5) 262 96 60.

Arkikatedra Bazilika (Cathedral)
Perhaps the best-known and arguably the most important building in Vilnius, the cathedral gives its name to the square on which it's situated, which is also the city's most popular meeting place. The cathedral site is thought to date back to pagan times when, so the story goes, a sacred pagan fire or altar was located here. It's generally agreed that Grand Duke Mindaugas built the first cathedral on this site after being baptised in 1251. The oldest parts of the current building date back to 1419, but the cathedral has been

Vilnius City

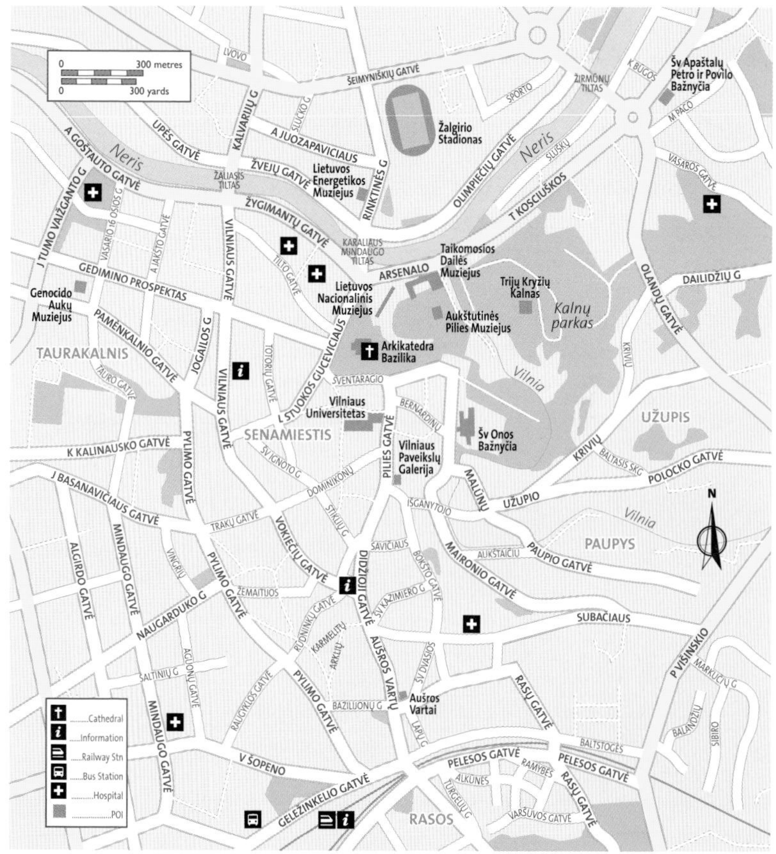

reconstructed and renovated several times following fire and natural damage, and features some Renaissance and Baroque elements. Much of its modern appearance dates from work carried out by the Lithuanian architect Laurynas Stuoka-Gucevičius (1753–98), considered to be the country's first professional architect, after severe damage by a storm in 1769, which destroyed the south tower of the façade. During the 1950s the Soviets closed the cathedral as a religious centre and used it as a picture gallery and organ concert venue. There were even plans at one point to turn it into a car repair workshop, such was the Soviet attitude towards the Church.

There are 11 chapels in this superb structure, of which the High Baroque St Casimir's Chapel, created in 1636 to house the silver sarcophagus of Lithuania's patron saint St Casimir, is

The cathedral with its free-standing belfry

The saints' statues on the façade were recreated after the originals were removed by the Soviets

regarded as a national treasure. The Wollowicz Chapel is also considered to be of high artistic merit. St Casimir's coffin was housed in here until it moved to the eponymous chapel in 1636. St Casimir features again on the roof of the building, along with sculptures of two other saints, St Stanislaus and St Helena. These represent the painstaking craft of restorers working from photographs to recreate the three original statues of the saints, which were torn down and discarded by the Soviets in 1950.

The belfry, a free-standing building 57m (187ft) high, was originally built as the defensive tower of the Lower Castle. The base of the tower dates from the 13th century and the round mid-section from the 14th century. Work began on transforming the tower into a belfry in 1522, and even though it has a mixture of Baroque (the first two tiers) and Classical (the third) styles, the result is harmonious. Ten of the bells in the belfry were cast between the 16th and 18th centuries by famous masters. In 1967, 17 new bells were added, and six more were received in 2002. Keep your ears peeled (no pun intended) for the tolls ringing out over the city every 15 minutes. The base of the tower is a popular meeting place, particularly among young lovers.

The imposing monument to Gediminas, the founder of Vilnius, dominates the southeastern corner of the square. Viewed against a

darkening sky the statue looks particularly dramatic. Immediately behind the cathedral a recreation of the former Royal Palace is being built on the site of the original building destroyed in 1801. Construction is due to finish in time for the country's 1,000th anniversary celebrations in 2009.
Katedros Aikštė 1. Tel: (8-5) 261 11 27.

Aukštutinės Pilies Muziejus (Higher Castle Museum)
All that remains of Gediminas Castle, built between the 13th and 15th centuries, is the three-storey defence tower known as Gediminas Tower (Gedimino Bokštas). Built in the Gothic style on an octagonal plan in red brick, the tower now houses the Higher Castle Museum with displays

THREE WOMEN WRITERS

Not only does Lithuania boast an unusually high number of female writing talents, Vilnius also plays host to a grand total of three significant monuments celebrating a trio of very different female writers. To date and rather unfortunately, virtually none of their work has been translated into English.

Žemaitė Arguably Lithuania's most famous female writer, Julija Beniuševičiūtė-Žymantienė, aka Žemaitė (1845–1921), was born in the village of Bukantė near Plungė in Žemaitija to an impoverished Polish-speaking family with aristocratic roots and aspirations. Forbidden to speak the vernacular Lithuanian as a child, Žemaitė made friends with the local Lithuanian-speaking peasants and soon became both fluent in the language and politically aware. With no formal education, the self-taught Žemaitė simultaneously brought up a family and worked on a farm whilst developing a writing career that ended with the completion of over 150 works, all based on the lives and struggles of peasant Lithuanian families. A large statue of Žemaitė stands in a small park between Gedimino 27 and 29.

Lazdynų Pelėda Translating somewhat mysteriously as Hazelnut Owl, Lazdynų Pelėda was the pen-name of the two sisters Marija Lastauskienė-Ivanauskaitė (1872–1957) and Sofija Pšibiliauskienė-Ivanauskaitė (1867–1926). Again, born into a Polish-speaking family at a time when it was considered terribly common to speak Lithuanian, their work (which was actually the work of Marija, with Sofija translating her sister's Polish into Lithuanian) was also politically driven and nationalistic in theme. A statue depicting the two sisters set in a strangely Egyptian style and called *Sesrys* (Sisters) can be found in another small park, this one at the point in the old town where Karmelitų and Arklių meet.

Salomėja Nėris Born in the small village of Kiršai to the southwest of Kaunas, Salomėja Nėris (real name Salomėja Bačinskaitė-Bučienė, 1904–45) was and still is one of the country's best-known and most controversial poets. Starting out as a teacher, in 1929 Nėris, who was already writing work of a nationalist, pro-Lithuanian nature, met and fell in love with the left-leaning Bronius Zubrickas, an event that changed her life completely as her poetry became increasingly pro-socialist in nature. Nėris sat out World War II in Russia, returning towards its end and dying of liver cancer in 1945. The winner of a Stalin Prize and a member of the so-called People's Parliament, Salomėja Nėris' pro-Lithuanian inter-war poems, along with the fact that she supposedly renounced her communism at the end of her life, has spared her from being labelled a traitor. Accordingly, the small Soviet-era figure of her head still stands on Vilniaus immediately south of St Catherine's Church (Šv Kotrynos Bažnyčia).

The Dawn Gate, a well-known Vilnius landmark that gives this street its name (Aušros Vartų)

on Vilnius' medieval fortification system, swords, armour and ancient coins. However, the best reason to come up here is for the spectacular views of the old town and beyond. *Arsenalo 5. Tel: (8-5) 261 74 53. Open: 10am–5pm. Admission charge.*

Aušros Vartai (Dawn Gate)

A famous symbol of the city of Vilnius, the Dawn Gate dates from the 16th century and was originally part of Vilnius' defensive walls. One of the finest Renaissance treats in the city, the gate was used to mark the eastern entrance to Vilnius. Since the expansion of the city, the gate now finds itself in the very centre. In 1671, the Carmelites from nearby St Theresa's built a chapel inside to house a holy image of the Virgin Mary. The most famous image of the Madonna in

Lithuanian art, the *Mother of Compassion* painting is supposed to possess special healing powers. Another interesting feature of this painting is that it is one of only five celebrated paintings of the Holy Mary in Lithuania where she is represented without the baby Jesus. The Madonna is considered to be a symbol of harmony and a special patron of Lithuania as she is worshipped by two religions, Catholics and Orthodox, and four nationalities, namely the Lithuanians, Poles, Russians and Belarusians. The chapel spreads across the top of the arch and you can see the image of the Virgin Mary when you approach the gate from the north as you walk up the hill. The interior of the chapel was refurbished in the neo-Classical style in 1829 and is well worth a look.

Aušros Vartų 12. Tel: (8-5) 212 35 13.

A cell at the Museum of Genocide Victims

Genocido Aukų Muziejus (Museum of Genocide Victims)

You get an inkling of what's to come as you approach this museum. The wall is covered with names carved into the stone. These are the victims of Stalin's terror; those who went into this prison and never come out. This former KGB prison, which also served at the Gestapo headquarters from 1941 to 1944, was in use until August 1991 when the KGB left Lithuania, and is more or less as it was at that time. The only difference is that there are printed explanations outside the rooms, describing their function. The jail was equipped in the autumn of 1940, soon after the Soviet Union occupied Lithuania. Beds and the occasional chair were added much later. Prior to that, inmates were packed into the cells up to 40 at a time, allowing only standing room.

As you go from cell to cell, a matter-of-fact description of the horrors that took place regularly in these cells keeps pace. There's a grim aspect to every cell. Visitors are taken through 19 common wards or cells as well as some of the specialised rooms, including the room of the officer on duty, with the equipment used in 1975, a watchroom with Soviet officers' uniforms and a tiny library that was made available to prisoners only in the

1980s. There's the cell for inquisitions, the padded cell, the isolation cell, and the water-torture or wet punishment cells. Here prisoners were left naked for hours on end, with frequent administrations of icy water keeping them awake. The passage stretches on bleakly, with cells off it to the right and left. Several contain themed exhibitions listing, with photographs, some of the KGB officers who presided over the jail or directed its operations. At the end of the corridor, there's a cell where prisoners were executed, with a glass-panelled floor and accompanying exhibition. It makes for a bizarre experience to realise that below your feet you can see the remains and intimate possessions of those who were held here.

On the ground floor find a detailed exhibition on the oppression of Lithuania under occupying regimes (1940–90). Material on and photographs of the anti-Soviet and anti-Nazi resistance are displayed, with stories and profiles of the participants. There is a particularly moving account of the Siberian deportations.
Aukų 2a. Tel: (8-5) 249 62 64.
Open: 10am–5pm, Sun 10am–3pm.
Closed: Mon. Admission charge.

Lietuvos Energetikos Muziejus (Lithuanian Energy Museum)

Located inside the capital's century-old former Central Power Plant, this fascinating museum is crammed full

Exhibits at the Lithuanian Energy Museum

of energy-related detritus from old cars to derelict steam boilers and a flashing model of the Ignalina Nuclear Power Plant (*see pp124–5*). The setting, of which much of the inside has been preserved, really adds something special to the whole effect. One of the city's better and more imaginative museums and well worth a visit.
Rinktinės 2. Tel: (8-5) 278 20 85.
Open: 8am–4pm. Closed: Sun & Mon.
Admission charge.

Lietuvos Nacionalinis Muziejus (Lithuanian National Museum)

A visit to this museum is an excellent way to get a handle on Lithuanian social history and culture. The extensive exhibits show the minutiae of daily living from the 13th century to

the present day, and are constantly updated. Some of the earliest Lithuanian coins, discovered as recently as 2002 around the site of the Lower Castle, are now on display at the museum.
Arsenalo 1. Tel: (8-5) 262 94 26. Open: 10am–5pm, Sun 10am–3pm. Closed: Mon. Admission charge.

Pilies Gatvė (Castle Street)

One of the oldest streets in Vilnius, this used to run from the southern gate of the Lower Castle all the way to the Town Hall. Nowadays Pilies runs only as far as the Russian Orthodox church St Paraskeva (Pyatnickaya), where it becomes Didžioji, then Aušros Vartų, leading up to the Dawn Gate.

Pilies is very much a commercial street, with some charming ancient lanes leading off it on both sides; to the west Skapo and Šv Jono (*see Walk, pp52–3*) and to the east Bernardinų, Šv Mykolo and Literatų. It's worth diving down some of these lanes as they contain some beautiful buildings and charming hidden courtyards. Some of the magnificent structures on Pilies still have their original stairways and elaborate decoration.

Trade was always the main function of this area and it is still Vilnius' most popular shopping neighbourhood. The street also contains several outdoor market stalls, selling a range of local and tourist-oriented items. Pilies has a wide range of upmarket

The Gothic St Anne's Church complex

shops, embassies, cultural centres and museums, as well as a plethora of cafés, bars and restaurants, which have outdoor seating during the summer.

Šv Apaštalų Petro ir Povilo Bažnyčia (Church of St Peter and St Paul)

Michael Casimir Pac, Governor of Vilnius and Grand Hetman (commander) of the Lithuanian armies, commissioned the building of this church in 1668 but unfortunately died before it was completed. The exterior of the church is impressive and attractive, but nothing to match the fabulous Baroque interior. Look to the right as you enter the church and you can see his tombstone embedded in the wall. Also note the figure of the Grim Reaper lurking in the alcove to the right just as you enter the church. The mind-boggling stucco figures that cover almost every internal surface number over two thousand and represent various Biblical, theological and battle scenes. An unusual and striking feature of the building interior is the huge ship-shaped chandelier that was made of brass and glass beads in Latvia, especially for the church. *Antakalnio 1. Tel: (8-5) 234 02 29.*

The Grim Reaper wails from an alcove in the Church of St Peter and St Paul

Šv Onos Bažnyčia (St Anne's Church)

The unusual group of buildings that includes St Anne's Church and the Bernardine Church on the eastern edge of the old town makes an extraordinary Gothic composition. St Anne's Church was built in the late 15th century and is considered the most famous late-Gothic building in Lithuania. According to local legend it was designed by Benedikt Rejt (1454–1536), who was also the architect of the Vladislav Hall in Hradčany, Prague. Its striking dark-red brick façade is a complex construction of 33 different varieties of bricks, combined to create a fine and elegant exterior. A much-quoted story describes how Napoleon Bonaparte was so impressed with the building that he wanted to take it back to Paris on the palm of his hand. The reality of his connection with the church is more prosaic; he used it to house his cavalry during his ill-fated march on Moscow in 1812.

Gothic brickwork on St Anne's Church

The **Bernardinų Bažnyčia** (Bernardine Church), in contrast to St Anne's, is one of the largest Gothic churches in Lithuania. Although predominantly Gothic in style, the Bernardine Church had some Renaissance and Baroque features added in the 17th and 18th centuries after it was damaged by fire and war. It was abandoned as a place of worship during Soviet occupation and handed over to the art academy next door, the Brothers of St Francis only returning in 1994. *Maironio 8/10.*

Taikomosios Dailės Muziejus (Applied Art Museum)

Housed in the Old Arsenal of the Lower Castle, this museum exhibits some truly outstanding examples of applied and religious art spanning the 14th to the 20th century.

Arsenalo 3a. Tel: (8-5) 262 80 80. Open: 11am–6pm, Sun 11am–4pm. Closed: Mon. Admission charge.

Trijų Kryžių Kalnas (Hill of Three Crosses)

High up on the hill on the opposite bank of the Vilnia River from Gediminas Castle, you can see three distinctive white crosses. Legend tells how centuries ago, seven Franciscan monks were crucified here and the bodies of four thrown into the Vilnia. Originally erected in the 17th century as symbols of mourning and hope, these crosses were removed and buried on Stalin's orders. The contemporary versions were rebuilt to the original specifications and erected in 1989. They are impressive both from a distance and up close, and it is worth the climb to the top to enjoy another excellent view of the old town.

Vilniaus Paveikslų Galerija (Vilnius Picture Gallery)

The former palace of the illustrious Chodkevičiai family features architectural elements from the 17th to the 19th century. Now a museum, it is full of wonderful examples of Lithuanian fine art including painting and sculpture from the 16th to the 19th century.

Didžioji 4. Tel: (8-5) 212 42 58. Open: noon–6pm, Sun noon–5pm. Closed: Mon. Admission charge.

Vilniaus Universitetas (Vilnius University)

The university is contained within four old town streets, Pilies to the east, Skapo to the north, Universiteto to the west and Šv Jono to the south and Daukanto Square. There are some other university buildings dotted around the old town, but it's this main area that contains the finest buildings and the most intense history.

One of the oldest universities in Eastern Europe, Vilnius University features examples of every major architectural style from the last 400 years. The beginnings of the university date from 1568, when Bishop Walerian Protasewicz (Lithuanian, Valerijonas Protasevičius) purchased a two-storey Gothic house in the area. This was later taken over by the Jesuit order which founded the university in 1579 and ran

Hill of Three Crosses

Evening sun lights up some of the fine university buildings

it for the next 200 years. From this relatively small building, the ensemble grew, with 12 more buildings added in the area. The Russians closed the university in 1832, and it was reopened only in 1919 after independence. A tremendous renovation effort was then carried out on the buildings. Completed in 1979, it made the university buildings among the best preserved in the city.

Each of the buildings has a number of wings, and these are set around courtyards of various dimensions. The complex is a wonderful place to soak up the atmosphere of the various courtyards and arcades. There are a range of halls and fine rooms inside these grand buildings that are well worth visiting, too, with the library affording one of the most impressive and interesting architectural sections of the university. A map of the complete ensemble at Universiteto 7 shows exactly where everything is.
Universiteto 3.

Vokiečių (German Street)

Another of the ancient streets of Vilnius, dating back to the 14th century, it was named after the German craftsmen and merchants who set up shop here. The street's heyday was in the 16th century, when the wealthiest merchants built the grandest masonry houses along it. Vokiečių continued to be a commercial centre up to the advent of World War II with, somewhat unusually, the large shops more likely to be found on the first floors of the big houses, and smaller ones tucked into courtyards and archways. After the war, the Soviets decided to redevelop the street and razed the half-destroyed eastern side of it to the ground, creating a grand wide road avenue with a grassy strip popular for strolling up and down along the middle. Over a period of time, the road was widened four times, and many monuments and fine buildings were destroyed in the process. With only the old buildings on the western side surviving, the contrast is very clear today.

One of the most impressive buildings is **Tyzenhaus**, the Wittinghoff estate at Number 28. This is an historic site with a grand building dating back to 1597. It was reconstructed a number of times over the years, but the magnificent Classical façade we see today was the work of Martin Knackfull, a popular period architect. The building was renovated most recently in the 1950s to repair the damage occasioned by World War II. Vokiečių is now littered with restaurants and bars, and is one of the city's most busy and popular streets.

ŽALIASIS TILTAS (THE GREEN BRIDGE)

An important river-crossing point since the first bridge was built here in 1536, the mildly controversial, 103m (338ft) long Green Bridge was built in 1952 to replace its predecessor destroyed during World War II. Incorporated into the original design at each of the bridge's four corners are a series of magnificent 3–4m (10–13ft) high socialist-realist sculptures representing agriculture (southwest), industry and construction (southeast), peace (northeast) and youth (northwest). One of only a handful of Soviet-era monuments left in the city, these slowly rusting masterpieces escaped removal when the rest of the city's communist monuments were removed, primarily because they bear no resemblance to anybody who actually ever lived, and therefore are not considered to be a direct insult to the nation. Now sadly cracked and rusting, it's likely that with nobody to look after them, the statues will soon be gone forever.

A sculpture on the Green Bridge

Walk: Old Vilnius

This easy but rewarding ramble charts a circular route around Vilnius' old town. It will take you through a mixture of main thoroughfares and quieter backstreets, which will enable you to get a quick sense of the history and atmosphere.

Time: Allow about three hours for the full walk, which will give you a chance to take the occasional break.

Distance: 3km (2 miles). Begin at Cathedral Square.

1 Katedros Aikštė (Cathedral Square)

There are 11 chapels within the vast cathedral worth visiting, and the bell tower next to the cathedral is one of the most popular meeting places (*see pp39–42*).

In the southeast corner is Pilies (Castle Street). Turn right down Skapo and into Universiteto to reach Vilnius University.

2 Vilniaus Universitetas (Vilnius University)

Founded in 1579, one of the oldest universities in Eastern Europe comprises many fine buildings (*see pp49–50*).

Walk across Universiteto to the Prezidentūra.

3 Prezidentūra (Presidential Palace)

Originally built for the city's Bishop in the 14th century, this gorgeous Classical white building has entertained various celebrated historical figures including Alexander I and Napoleon Bonaparte. It now contains the President's offices.

Continue along Universiteto, then turn left down Šv Jono and right to rejoin Pilies. Pilies becomes Didžioji. Continue up the hill until you reach the Town Hall.

4 Rotušė (Town Hall)

Now housing the Artists' Palace, this Classical structure was a theatre until 1924 when it became the Lithuanian Art Museum under Soviet occupation.

Take the road off to the southeast corner and turn on to Šv Kazimiero.

5 Šv Kazimiero Bažnyčia (St Casimir's Church)

Used as a grain store by Napoleon's troops in 1812, the church was converted into a cathedral by the Russians in 1864, then into a Museum of Atheism. It was returned to its original use after independence.

Walk down Aušros Vartų until you reach the Dawn Gate.

6 Aušros Vartai (Dawn Gate)

This famous gate is one of the city's primary landmarks (*see pp43–4*).

Go through the Dawn Gate, turn right down Bazilijonų, take the first right down Visų Šventųjų, and then third right down Rudninkų. Turn left into Vokiečių.

7 Vokiečių

You can guess at this street's former glory from the fine buildings that remain on the eastern side (*see pp50–51*).

At the end of Vokiečių head down Vilniaus and continue along the road until it culminates at Gedimino.

8 Gedimino (Gediminas Avenue)

Built towards the end of the 19th century as a Russian showcase, Gedimino is the main shopping street.

*Heading east down the hill past the Sąjūdis Museum (*see p15*) brings you back to the start of the walk.*

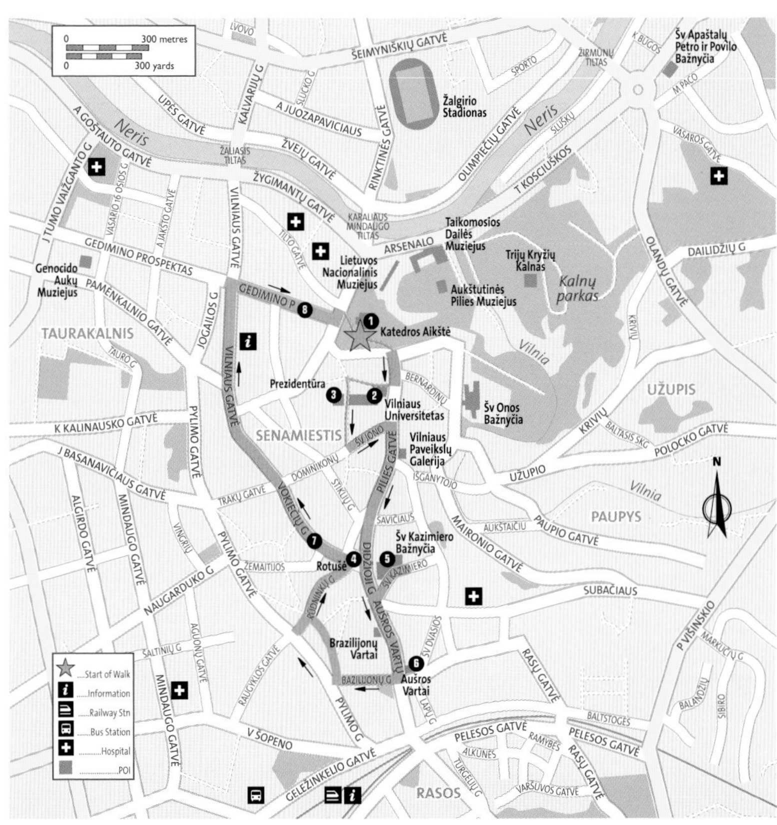

Walk: Scenic Vilnius

This is more of a scenic walk – punctuated with some important sights – than a purely cultural experience. It is a walk that is geared towards vistas, both along the River Neris and out over the city.

Time: Allow three hours.

Distance: 4km ($2\frac{1}{2}$ miles).

Start the walk at the Green Bridge on the Šnipiskės side.

1 Žaliasis Tiltas (Green Bridge)

The Green Bridge (*see box p51*) links the city centre to the one-time Jewish district and now rapidly expanding business area of Šnipiskės north of the Neris River. The river is the second biggest in Lithuania, but unfortunately it's also one of the most polluted, so don't be tempted to swim or fish in it.

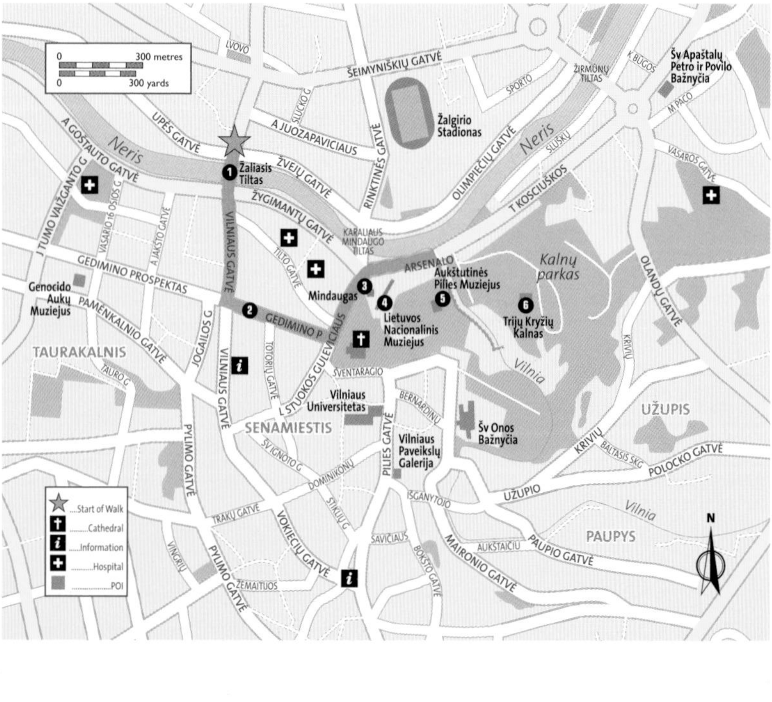

Cross over the river and head straight up Vilniaus, past the extraordinary 1974 Opera and Ballet Theatre on your right until you reach the junction of Gedimino.

2 Gedimino (Gediminas Avenue)

This street is now named after the Lithuanian Grand Duke after a string of monikers including its last name honouring Lenin. After a major facelift, Gedimino is now *the* street to shop in and is a popular place for locals to take a stroll on warm summer days. Time spent on Gedimino will vary depending on the needs and energy of the walkers. Gedimino contains everything from outdoor cafés to modern shopping centres to the haunting Museum of Genocide Victims (*see pp44–5*).
Head east down Gedimino as far as the cathedral.

3 Mindaugas

At the front of the cathedral (*see pp39–42*) follow the tree-lined path to the north, past three small and rather bizarre-looking statues on the right until you reach an even more peculiar-looking monument bearing an uncanny resemblance to Davros from the BBC science fiction television series *Doctor Who*. Unveiled on 6 July 2003 and the work of R Midvikis, closer inspection reveals the statue to be none other than Lithuania's one and only crowned king, Mindaugas.
Directly behind Mindaugas find the entrance to the Lithuanian National Museum.

4 Lietuvos Nacionalinis Muziejus (Lithuanian National Museum)

There is a huge collection of items in this museum (*see pp45–6*), ranging from books, coins, weapons and prints to pieces of architectural interest, folk art and findings from the mass graves of the soldiers of Napoleon's retreating army. You certainly come away with a better feel of what Lithuania and its people are all about.
Just next door to the museum is the entrance to the funicular railway that will take you up to the Higher Castle.

5 Aukštutinės Pilies Muziejus (Higher Castle Museum)

Explore the castle ruins and the tower (*see pp42–3*), but don't miss the fabulous view over the city. Make your way back down the hill on foot along the spiral, cobbled path, but make sure you're wearing shoes with the ability to grip. Even when dry, the smooth cobbles are slightly slippery.
Take a right when leaving the museum and follow the Neris River east over the Vilnia River before taking a right that takes you up a series of long steep roads and paths to reach the Hill of Three Crosses (Trijų Kryžių Kalnas). Clamber up to the crosses themselves and reward yourself with one of the best views of the city you'll find anywhere.

6 Trijų Kryžių Kalnas (Hill of Three Crosses)

For more information about the Hill of Three Crosses, see p49.

Užupis

Immediately east of the old town across the River Vilnia is the so-called Republic of Užupis. First mentioned in the 16th century, Užupis was the first part of the city to grow outside the city walls. Enjoying a post-independence reputation as the home of Vilnius' students, poets, romantics and artists, Užupis has over the last few years fallen victim to a predictable gentrification and the soaring rent and property prices that go with the phenomenon. A one-time crumbling mess, Užupis' resemblance to Havana has long since been replaced with a much slicker look.

Užupis does remain, however, a centre for non-conventional ideas. Not only does it have its own road signs, but also its own Constitution, President, Ministers, an Ambassador in Moscow, and its own public holidays. The most popular of these is on 1 April, Užupis' Day of Independence, when border guards stop visitors and offer *Užupio Respublika* (Republic of Užupis) stamps in their passports. Other holidays in Užupis include the 24 July Day of the River, the Night of the Flowers on 15 August and the unforgettable Day of the Idiot on 21 September.

In the spiritual centre of Užupis, where the streets of Malūnų, Paupio and Užupio intersect, there's a tall pillar on which sits the statue of the famous Užupis Angel – the work of local sculptor R Vilčiauskas – unveiled on 1 April 2002. Looking rather fine and blowing a large trumpet, the angel caused the Dalai Lama in 2001,

Graffiti in the bohemian 'Republic' of Užupis

A close-up of the Užupis Angel

who was in Vilnius before the project was completed, to comment that he wished the trumpet would sound throughout the world. The angel was 'hatched' from a large concrete egg that graced the pillar whilst money for the angel was raised, and can now be found just south of the old town in the little square at the junctions of Pylimo, Raugyklos and Šv Stepono. The egg was recently painted to resemble a traditional Lithuanian Easter egg by the Lithuanian artist Lijana Turskytė.

The old Bernardine Cemetery (Bernadinų Kapinės) that stretches along the steep riverside at the southeastern end of the district at Žvirgždyno 3 has become something of a mystical location in Užupis. Burials began here in 1810, and during the 1863 Uprising, rebels hid their weapons here. The gravestones of many Vilnius University professors and scientists can be found in this peaceful spot. Close to the Bernardine Church and Cemetery is the Fluxus Bridge, named after the group that tried to blow up the bridge in order, somehow, to destroy the border between art and life.

As Užupis continues to grow in stature, so the local artists who rent the once-cheap workshops and galleries are being forced out. Several still remain, however, and the area is well worth a visit. There are also some fairly decent restaurants and bars scattered around.

EXCERPTS FROM THE UŽUPIS CONSTITUTION

- Man has the right to live beside the River [Vilna], and the Vilna has the right to flow beside the man
- Man has the right to be not famous or unknown
- Man has the right to be loved, but not necessarily
- Man has the right to love and care for a cat
- A cat is not obliged to love its owner but during hard times it is obliged to help the owner
- Man has the right to care for a dog until one of them passes away

Around Vilnius

For travellers with plenty of time on their hands while in Vilnius, there are many varied sights to explore on the outskirts of the city. Some are close enough to walk to, others a short bus ride away. All are reachable by car. Guided bus tours to Trakai and Europos Parkas generally leave in the morning and take around three and a half hours. They'll pick you up and return you to your hotel.

Belmontas

What started as a tiny riverside restaurant next to a babbling brook back in 2001 has turned into something altogether larger and more fun, and it's less than 15 minutes east of the city centre. Built on the site of a 19th-century water mill, Belmontas offers the full-on traditional Lithuanian folk experience including three restaurants selling a range of classic local dishes, saunas, banquet halls, waterfalls and even a museum dedicated to traditional Lithuanian arts and crafts.
www.belmontas.lt

Paneriai

A very different experience from visiting the above, Paneriai (or Ponar as it was and still is known to the Jews) is located about 10km (6¼ miles) northwest of the centre of the city. This infamous village on the edge of a forest is where the Nazis and their Lithuanian henchmen murdered over 100,000 civilians during World War II. Among those murdered and thrown into oil storage pits were people brought from all over Europe. The area where the killings took place is a 1km (⅔-mile) walk into the woods from Paneriai's

Chapel in Paneriai cemetery

tiny train station. There are two stones marking the entrance to the site, which were erected after the war by the communists and simply tabulate the 'Soviet citizens' who were murdered. The reality was that over 70 per cent of the people murdered here were Jews, and the memorial erected in 1990 makes this clear with its inscription in Hebrew. It's still possible to see the remains of the barracks and the pits.

To get to Paneriai take a Kaunas-, Trakai-, Šeštokai- or Varėna-bound train from Vilnius. From the Paneriai station, turn right onto Agrastų, and follow the road for about 1km (2/3 mile) until you reach the forest and the first of the memorials. By car, take Savanorių west out of the city until you reach the E28 highway and follow the signs from there.

Panerių Memorialinis Muziejus (Paneriai Memorial Museum)
This museum has a small but graphically informative display showing the atrocities that happened here and the chilling subsequent cover-up attempt by the Nazis. The building was purpose-built in 1965.
Agrastų 15, Paneriai. Tel: (8-5) 260 20 01. Open: call in advance to arrange. Admission charge.

Around Vilnius

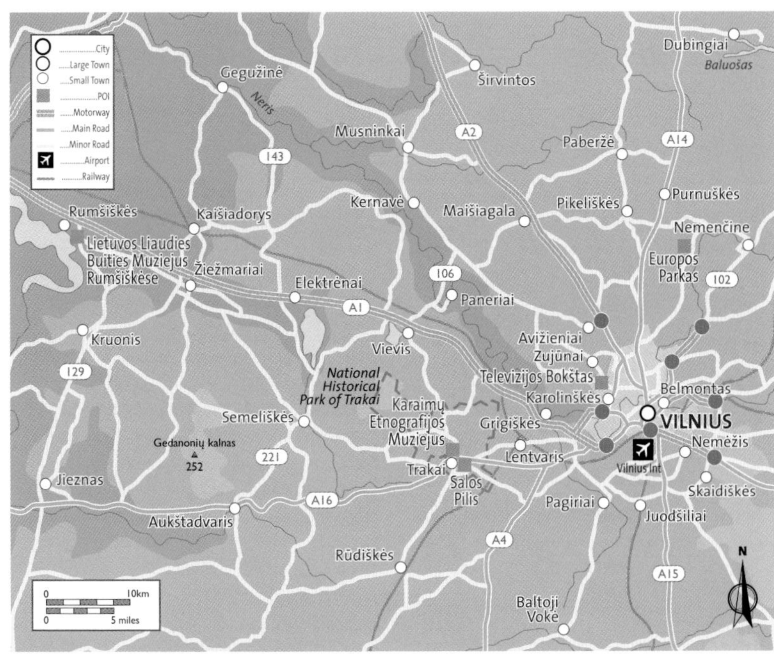

Rumšiškės

At just over 80km (50 miles) west of the capital along the best road in the country (and a mere 20km/12 miles east of Kaunas along the same highway), Rumšiškės is a relatively close and rewarding day-trip from either city. The village itself has an extremely attractive setting on the banks of the Nemunas River. Archaeologists have found bronze artefacts in the area dating from the 13th to the 16th centuries, but the real attraction is just outside the village in the large open-air museum.

Lietuvos Liaudies Buities Muziejus Rumšiškėse (Rumšiškės Open-air Museum of Lithuania)

Spread over 176ha (435 acres) of luscious rolling country, this exemplary ethnographic park features workshops, cottages, schools and farm buildings from the different regions of the country, painstakingly taken apart and reassembled here. These assorted structures represent the most characteristic and stylistic features of buildings from different historical eras. The huge collection of over 80,000 items includes furniture, household items, beehives, orchards and artefacts. The aim of the museum is to illustrate the way of life, work and traditions of the Lithuanian people, both urban and rural, over the last hundred years. To get there, take the country's main A1 highway, get off at the Rumšiškės junction and follow the signs.

Tel: (8-346) 473 92. Open: 10am–6pm. Closed: Mon. Admission charge.

Televizijos Bokštas (Television Tower)

Although the building itself is not one of outstanding architectural note, it's the historical associations that make Vilnius' Television Tower in the northwestern housing district of Karoliniškės an interesting place to visit. On 13 January 1991, in an attempt to prevent Lithuania achieving its independence, Soviet tanks surrounded the Television Tower and launched an attack on the civilians who were protesting there, leaving a total of 14 dead. There are poignant monuments outside the tower and inside is a small exhibition of photographs. The tower itself, at 326m (1,070ft), is higher than the Eiffel Tower. A café inside the 270m (886ft) high observation deck offers spectacular views of the city.

THE KARAITE

The Lithuanian Karaite (a Jewish group) originally came from the Byzantine Empire in Mesopotamia in the 8th century, and then moved into the Crimean Peninsula, from where Grand Duke Vytautas brought them to Trakai as slaves in the 15th century. They were soon elevated to the status of personal guards to the Grand Duke. Other Karaite followed, and a small community was formed that still exists in the town today. The word Karaite comes originally from the Arabic and Hebrew word *kara*, meaning 'to read from the scriptures'. Of the 250 Karaite still living in Lithuania, most live in Trakai.

The Island Castle in Trakai

Sausio 13-osios 10. Tel: (8-5) 252 53 33. Open: 10am–9pm. Admission charge.

Trakai

Some 28km (17 miles) west of Vilnius, Trakai is both a region and the name of the main town in the region. The Trakai district, with a population of around 38,000, is well known for its lakes, which number over 300, as well as over 200 agricultural, natural and cultural monuments. Trakai is famous both within Lithuania and abroad for its beautiful surroundings, lakes, historic sights and charming village. There's a concentration of tourist shops and cafés in the town centre, from where you can walk across various islands to reach the splendid Island Castle. It's a quiet place with a somewhat otherworldly air.

Trakai was founded in the late 14th century by Grand Duke Kęstutis, when he moved from Old Trakai and took up residence in the peninsular castle built between the lakes of Luka and Galvė. Further buildings were constructed and, in time, a whole settlement grew around the castle protected by the surrounding hills. During the late 14th and 15th centuries, Trakai developed as a place of huge strategic importance, becoming both the administrative and political capital of Lithuania. Historically, Trakai has been unique in Lithuania for its multicultural character. This was partly due to Grand Duke Vytautas, who brought Karaite

Typical Karaite houses with three windows

(Lithuanian, *Karaimai*) and Sunni Muslim Tartar families to Lithuania in the 15th century. In the 16th century, a number of Jewish families settled and added to the mix. Today Trakai prides itself on the richness and variety of its culture. Included within the territory are both the National Historical Park of Trakai and the Aukštadvaris Regional Park.

The Tourist Information Centre here should be one of your first ports of call in the town. The centre has a plethora of information and maps, as well as extremely helpful and informative staff.

Tourist Information Centre. Vytauto 69. Tel: (8-528) 51 934. www.trakai.lt

Karaimų Etnografijos Muziejus (Karaite Ethnographic Museum)
Inside this tiny building find a treasure trove of exhibits including old photographs, scriptures, jewellery, classic Karaite pointed shoes and some beautiful and ornate weapons. Current estimates put the total Karaite population in Lithuania at around 250.

The **Kenesa (Karaite Prayer House)** just north of the museum (*Karaimų 30*) dates from the 18th century and is distinctively Eastern in style. Unless you're lucky enough to find a ceremony taking place, you'll almost certainly find it locked.

Museum: Karaimų 22. Tel: (8-528) 55 286. Open: 10am–6pm. Closed: Mon & Tue. Admission charge.

Karaimų (Karaite Street)
Essentially Trakai's main street, running north–south in the northern part of the town and named after the many Karaite who still live along it. The Karaite are known as both excellent craftsmen and for their superb gardening and agricultural skills. A traditional Lithuanian Karaite house, of which many examples can be see along here, is a one-floor dwelling notable for having three windows at the front, one window for God, one for Duke Vytautas and the third for the Karaite themselves.

The street also boasts a fine Karaite restaurant, **Kybynlar** (*see p169*), serving a range of traditional Karaite dishes, including the best example you'll find anywhere of the classic *kibinai* (decorated pastry cases stuffed with a mixture of chopped meat and onions and mixed together with a rich, greasy gravy).

National Historical Park of Trakai
The National Historical Park of Trakai was set up in 1991 and is the only historical park in the country. Made up of 32 lakes, a bird sanctuary, three hydrographical reserves and two cultural reserves, it covers an area of over 8,000ha (19,770 acres) and includes, in addition to the above, the cultural landscape reserve of Užutrakis and the urban reserve of Trakai old town. Find out more from the local tourist information centre (*see opposite*).

Salos Pilis (Island Castle)
The most striking building in Trakai is the Island Castle, the only insular castle in Lithuania and the only water castle in Eastern Europe. It was built by the Lithuanian Grand Dukes Kęstutis and Vytautas at the end of the 14th and the beginning of the 15th centuries to a very unusual ground plan and was set strategically on a relatively inaccessible island in Lake Galvė to withstand attacks from the Teutonic Knights. After the joint Polish-Lithuanian victory over the Teutonic Order at the Battle of Žalgiris in 1410, the Island Castle became the summer residence of the rulers of the Great Duchy of Lithuania. This was the castle's heyday. Over the ensuing centuries, it suffered great damage and was left in ruins. However, restoration started in the 1950s during the Soviet era, and work continues today.

The castle complex is built over three separate islands, and includes a fortress which links to the Gothic Ducal Palace, surrounded by a defensive wall. The main landmark of the complex is the five-storey turret (*donjon*), which rises to 25m (82ft). There are wooden stairways and balconies connecting the palace to the castle, and one of the huge halls on the first floor is still used for concerts and other performances. Some of the other buildings have been converted, one housing an eclectic

Part of the bridge to Trakai's Island Castle

collection of historical objects and pictures tracing the building's past. The Island Castle is reached from the town across a wooden bridge, then over the tiny Karvinė Island and across another wooden bridge.

Pilies Sala. Tel. (8-528) 53 946.
Open: 10am–7pm. Admission charge.

Trakai boat trip

Trakai is located on a thin peninsula among three lakes, Galvė, Luka and Totoriškių. Although a wonderful place to just wander around, you get a whole different perspective if you explore it from the water. It's possible to rent your own rowing or paddle boat on Lake Galvė, the largest of the three lakes. You can also take a guided yacht trip, although you're best to rent your own so long as you feel confident and wear a life jacket. There are a number of outlets renting a variety of boats to the south of the Island Castle on the lake shore, as well as around the first bridge that leads to the Island Castle. Bartering with the boat owners can get you a reasonable price for an hour's rental. Expect to pay up to three times as much for a yacht as for a rowboat or a canoe.

Touring by boat is a great way to see the Island Castle. Lake Galvė, on which the Island Castle sits, is the most spectacular of the lakes in this area. At 46.7m (153ft) deep and covering an area of 361ha (892 acres), it's both the largest and deepest lake in the region. It's also a designated nature reserve, made up of many peninsulas and bays coming in various shapes and sizes. There are 21 islands on Galvė, most having legends connected to them. Two islands are close to the centre of the lake, the Isle of Wailing (Rauda Sala) and Valka. In the past, criminals sentenced to death would be taken to Valka, and their relatives to Rauda Sala, from where they could grimly observe their loved one wait for death. Castle Island is the largest of the lake's islands.

In the summer months, a lake steamer makes frequent trips from the Island Castle to the northern end of Lake Galvė. The lake is also a popular place for hot-air ballooning, paragliding and canoeing, and there are often competitions taking place here in the summer. Island Castle is also a hugely popular backdrop for photographs of Lithuanian newly-weds. Sailing competitions and national and international rowing competitions also take place here. If you're feeling adventurous and want to go cruising a bit further afield, head for the nearby Užutrakis Palace, which has a lovely park and is a great place to stop for a walk and a picnic.

The amazing Island Castle is the only water castle in Eastern Europe

The centre of Europe?

There are multitudes of destinations fighting for the recognition – and subsequent influx of tourists that comes with it – of being the exact centre of Europe, including points in the Czech Republic, Ukraine and Lithuania. Lithuania's claim that the precise centre of Europe is 26km (16 miles) north of Vilnius was verified by the French National Geographic Institute in 1989, a fact that the Lithuanians seem to think gives them the true title.

The scientifically calculated centre of Europe is marked by this simple pillar

Europos Centro Muziejus (Centre of Europe Museum)

If you head north out of Vilnius on the A14 highway in the direction of Molėtai, near the village of Purnuškės, at 54° 51′ North latitude, 25° 19′ East longitude to be exact, you will find the place that all the fuss is about. While the site isn't particularly exciting, it's worth a visit for the kudos it brings. There's a memorial stone, an information centre and museum. Visitors can also get certificates to verify that they have been to the centre of Europe.
26km (16 miles) from Vilnius, towards Molėtai, behind Purnuškės village, Bernotai Mound. Open: 9am–sunset. Admission charge.

Europos Parkas (Europe Park)

A more interesting commemoration of the centre of Europe status is Europos Parkas, a large sculpture park located 14km (8¾ miles) south of the actual point. This highly original art museum and park was founded in 1991 by the then 23-year-old art student Gintaras Karosas. Located in a forest 19km (12 miles) north of Vilnius city, the park was established with the aim of underlining the area's

Some of the sculptures are interactive

status by using the language of art and, somehow, by expressing the centre of Europe through the miscellaneous works on display. The only international contemporary sculpture park in Lithuania, the 55ha (136-acre) Europos Parkas displays contemporary work by a variety of artists from over 30 countries including Canada, Egypt, Great Britain, Poland, the USA and, of course, Lithuania. The sculptures, representing different cultural traditions and international backgrounds, are on display all year round, with new ones being added from time to time. In 2005, the collection on display in the park reached over 100 pieces.

The park exhibits large-scale works by famous contemporary artists, including Magdalena Abakanowicz, Sol LeWitt and Dennis Oppenheim. The largest, and possibly the most well known, of the pieces is the sculpture *LNK Infotree*, created by Karosas himself. Made of hundreds of used television sets to create a labyrinth in tree form, the sculpture takes up more than 3,135sq m (33,740sq ft) of space. It's not surprising that this supposedly sly dig at the absurdities of communism has been officially registered in *Guinness World Records* as the largest work of art made from televisions in the world. The pieces *Chair Pool* and *Drinking Structure with Exposed Kidney Pool*, both by Dennis Oppenheim of the USA, are also well known. *Chair Pool*, as its name indicates, is a huge chair with a pool in the seat.

The overall setting of the area itself is outstanding, with a reservoir, park and wooded hills providing a stunning backdrop for the intriguing sculptures. The museum also has a small restaurant, gift shop and post office.

Joneikiškiai village. Tel: (8-5) 237 70 77. Open: 9am–sunset. Admission charge.

Dennis Oppenheim's *Chair Pool*

Southern Lithuania

*The combination of great natural beauty and some fortunate geological features has resulted in a spate of spa towns in Lithuania's picturesque south. Perhaps the most popular of the resort towns is Druskininkai, on the banks of the Nemunas River. The local mud and mineral springs are believed to have curative powers. The other highly popular resort is Birštonas, where mineral water is the focal point of treatments. There is something to draw nature lovers as well, in the form of the Žuvintas Strict State Reserve (*see pp72–3*).*

Druskininkai

One of the oldest and best-known spas and recreational resorts in Eastern Europe, Druskininkai is beautifully located on the banks of the mighty Nemunas River, very near the borders of both Poland and Belarus, about 120km (75 miles) southwest of Vilnius, and is surrounded by pine forests filling the air with a wonderfully clean, fresh scent. An area rich in natural springs featuring water with a high salt content, the word Druskininkai translates as 'Salt Man' or 'Salt Worker', a name used to describe anyone involved in the extraction, sale or delivery of salt.

Verdant parkland on the edge of Lake Druskonis

One of the central features of Druskininkai is Lake Druskonis (Druskonio Ežeras), bordered on its northern side by Čiurlionio, the main road that runs right the way through the resort. The town itself is spread over quite a wide area made up of parks and gardens and dotted with lakes. It has a peaceful and unhurried atmosphere, making it an ideal place to spend a few days enjoying the scenery, walking in the surrounding forests and taking advantage of one of the many spa treatments available in the resort.

Traces of habitation going back to the Mesolithic and Neolithic eras have been found in the area. Other archaeological findings include the remains of a defensive castle at the confluence of the Nemunas and Ratnyčia Rivers. The castle is believed to date from the 13th century, when the

Southern Lithuania

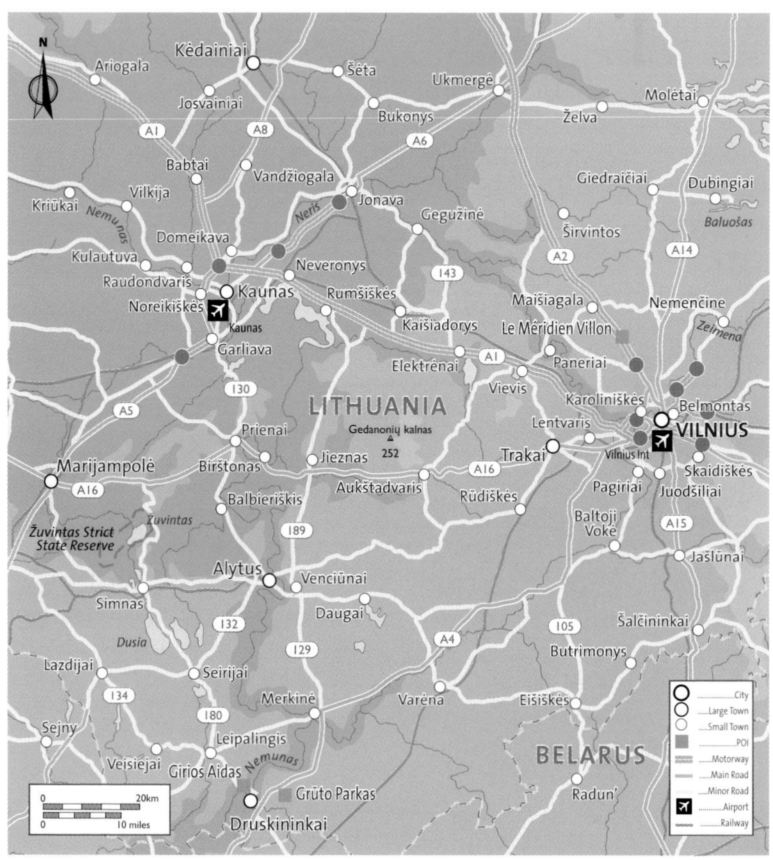

still pagan Lithuanians were fighting against the Teutonic Order.

The first mention of Druskininkai in written records occurs in the Lithuanian *Metrics* of 1596. The curative powers of the springs near the Nemunas River were discovered by the villagers when they noticed that their ulcerous legs healed faster after they had waded in the waters of the springs. However, it was Pranas Sūrutis, a folk doctor in the 18th century, who was the first to use the mineral springs specifically for healing purposes.

Although Druskininkai did not officially become a spa until 1837, in 1790 King Stanislaus Augustus (Polish, Stanisław Antoni Poniatowski) ordered that the health-giving properties of the mineral waters of Druskininkai be investigated, and in 1794 it was announced by decree that the place was a curative locality. Later, Professor I Fonberg of Vilnius University published his research on the chemical composition of the mineral water here in 1835. It was this data that made Tsar Nikolai I grant permission for the area to be developed as a spa in 1837.

The development of Druskininkai was assisted by the proximity of the railway line connecting Warsaw and St Petersburg, which opened in 1862. Thanks to this and the official recognition of the special nature of the place, Druskininkai was granted town status. After a brief spell as Poland's number one spa resort between the wars, Druskininkai was returned to (Soviet) Lithuania in 1945. Reconstructive work was carried out in the 1950s, and the resort was tailored during the time of Soviet occupation for the mass treatment of patients from the USSR.

Nowadays there are about a dozen sanatoria providing treatments for virtually all known diseases, with all the experience, research and expertise accumulated over the years. The main treatments use local mineral waters, salt and curative mud, which are ranked among the best in Europe. But with its outstanding microclimate, peaceful setting, pristine lakes and rivers, dunes and pine forests, and pure, scented air, you cannot but leave here

DRUSKININKAI ARCHITECTURE

Architecturally there's no one predominant style in the town, being like many Lithuanian destinations the sum of its previous inhabitants. Magnificent wooden villas from the beginning of the 20th century rub shoulders with daring Soviet-era buildings resembling spaceships. Occasional treats pop up, such as the diminutive and charming Russian Orthodox Church. This ornate and flamboyant wooden building with bright blue spires and purple-hued domes sits serenely in the middle of a leafy reservation circled by the resort's traffic. It's worth taking a look at the interior, which is also very much of the same period. Those who have never visited a Russian Orthodox place of worship may wonder where the seating is. Unlike the Catholic Church, which long since abandoned prolonged standing up during masses, the Russian Orthodox Church still favours this altogether more pious form of worshipping.

feeling refreshed and revitalised, whether you indulge in the spa experience or not. Druskininkai is, simply, a very special place to visit.

Girios Aidas (Echo of the Forest)
If you head out of town along Čiurlionio about 1.5km (1 mile) towards Merkinė you will come to this extraordinary exhibition housed in a fantastical wooden construction and surrounded by eccentric wooden sculptures at every turn. Wooden snakes lie in the grass, giants stand as pillars of the house, and sculptures of birds and animals are tucked into the

The Russian Orthodox Church in Druskininkai

hollows of trees. Dwarves, witches and other fantasy figures are dotted around the grounds. Inside, the exhibition is divided into different sections, and parts of the local ecosystem, trees, animals and birds are examined. An imaginative, fun and educational place to visit.
Čiurlionio 116. Tel: (8-313) 53 901. Open: 10am–6pm. Closed: Mon & Tue. Admission charge.

Miesto Muziejus (City Museum)
At the turreted Villa Linksma (Happy Villa) built in the early 20th century, the Miesto Muziejus (City Museum) has an interesting collection of pictures and other exhibits showing the history of the town from its earliest days through to the 21st century.
Čiurlionio 59. Tel: (8-313) 51 024. Open: 11am–5pm. Closed: Sun. Admission charge.

MK Čiurlionio Memorialininis Muziejus (MK Čiurlionis Memorial Museum)
As you may have gathered from the naming of the town's main street, Mikalojus Konstantinas Čiurlionis (1875–1911), Lithuania's most famous painter and composer, had a strong connection with Druskininkai, having spent part of his early life here. It's therefore fitting that the town should have a museum in his honour. Providing the visitor with a detailed insight into the composer's life, the museum was established in the house where the Čiurlionis family lived. The family had two small houses, and there's also a recreation of the wooden house that his father bought in the town. It's filled with 19th-century memorabilia as well as the piano Čiurlionis' patron Count Oginski gave him in 1899 on his graduation from the Warsaw Conservatoire. There is also an interesting display of photographs of various members of the Čiurlionis family. Classical concerts are held in the garden here in summer.
Čiurlionio 35. Tel: (8-313) 51 131. Open: 11am–5pm. Closed: Mon. Admission charge.

Žuvintas Strict State Reserve
In addition to Lithuania's national and regional parks, the country also has

ČIURLIONIS

Lithuania's undisputed creative genius, Mikalojus Konstantinas Čiurlionis was born into a Polish-speaking family in Varėna in 1875. The author of Lithuania's first symphony *Miške* (*In The Forest*, 1901), Čiurlionis not only wrote music but was also a serious painter (some argue that he even went so far as to invent Abstract art), conductor, photographer and a leading provocateur in the Lithuanian independence movement. Married to the writer Sofija Kymantaitė, with whom he had a daughter, Čiurlionis was a shy depressive who died at the early age of 35 in 1911. The house in which he grew up in Druskininkai is now a museum (*see above*) and his paintings can be seen on display in the museum that bears his name in Kaunas (*see p81*).

four so-called Strict State Reserves, of which the Žuvintas Strict State Reserve just east of the city of Alytus is one of the most attractive. Established in 1937, mainly through the efforts of the naturalist Tadas Ivanauskas, the reserve incorporates Lake Žuvintas and part of the Bukta Forest, and is an important wetland area. It seeks to preserve the area's delicate ecosystem and wildlife, especially the birdlife of the lake and surrounding wetlands.

Spread over an area of 5,440ha (13,440 acres), the reserve is 72 per cent wetland and 13 per cent lake. The lake has shallow and silty waters full of submerged plants that thrive in this type of water. There are also many floating islets called *kiniai*. Next to the lake are huge areas of reeds and sedge, particularly favoured by wading birds, as well as two tracts of raised bogs.

The reserve is famed for its birdlife, with an amazing 255 registered species. Lake Žuvintas provides a nesting ground for many aquatic birds. The lake is known as the cradle of Lithuanian swans, because it's from here that they spread to other Lithuanian lakes. Huge flocks of thousands of migrating cranes and geese stop off here to rest every year in season, which is quite a sight to behold.

In the last few decades, the lake has become very 'old', a phenomenon caused by poor water-level control and the draining of huge amounts of fertilisers and other chemical and organic substances into the lake from surrounding fields. Plans to establish a biosphere reserve in the lake have been discussed, which would be a step in the right direction to save the area's ecosystem and birdlife.

Žuvintas Strict State Reserve Visitors' Centre. Aleknonys village.
Tel: (8-315) 49 540. www.zuvintas.lt

This precarious walkway gives you a good view of Lake Žuvintas

Spa towns

A popular destination for those seeking to improve their health or wishing to rejuvenate mind, body or spirit, Lithuania has enjoyed a great spa tradition for centuries. While many towns in the country offer spa treatments, the towns of Druskininkai and Birštonas are the most popular of the spa resorts. Famous for their mineral springs, Druskininkai and Birštonas have the added attraction of being set in picturesque surroundings. Palanga is another well-known retreat destination out of season, but suffers from an enormous influx of 24-hour party people during the summer.

Druskininkai

Druskininkai (*see pp68–72*), in the south of Lithuania, is the biggest and oldest health resort in the country. The local mud and mineral springs here are well known for their curative powers.

Having taken the waters, spa visitors enjoy the peaceful surroundings

Additionally, the town's location, 90m (295ft) above sea level on the right bank of the River Nemunas and surrounded by pine forests, ensures that the air is always clean and fresh. The healing properties of Druskininkai's mineral water springs were first observed in the early 18th century. Throughout the 19th and 20th centuries, many wooden villas and small sanatoria were built, most of them specialising in mud and climate therapies. Heart, digestion and nervous diseases are only a few of the ailments treated here. The local mineral water is central to the treatments, with patients drinking mineral water, undergoing mineral water-bath treatments, and taking mineral water inhalations. Rapid development in recent years has seen many high-standard facilities opening up in this area. Druskininkai's remarkably attractive and diverse surroundings make it an ideal town for walking and cycling around, for those who would like to combine their health stint with these gentle activities. *www.druskininkai.lt*

Birštonas

The other highly popular health resort is Birštonas, tucked inside a loop of

International flags flutter at the entrance to one of Druskininkai's spas

the Nemunas River some 80km (50 miles) west of Vilnius. When Druskininkai was annexed by Poland between the wars, Birštonas' popularity among Lithuanians as well as people from other nations rose quickly. Mineral water is the focal point of treatments here as well. Drinking, bathing and inhalations are included in the treatment of patients with digestive disorders, blood circulation problems, kidney and respiratory diseases. The sanatoria in Birštonas are open all year round. The town itself is beautiful, containing a museum of local teachings, a rowing station and a decent tourist information centre. Birštonas' biennial Jazz Festival, held in early spring, attracts big crowds.
www.birstonas.lt

Neringa and Palanga

Neringa and Palanga (*see pp94–7*) on the Baltic coastline are also popular resorts. Palanga is a climatic and mud-therapy resort with beaches by the Baltic Sea, but it's very busy from June to August. Neringa is a bit quieter than Palanga. A long, narrow strip of sand and a UNESCO World Heritage Site, Neringa's most popular sanatorium is Ąžuolynas (*www.hotelazuolynas.lt*) in the small town of Juodkrantė.
www.neringa.lt
www.palanga.lt

Le Méridien Villon

Another spa resort worth mentioning is the upmarket, elegant Le Méridien Villon inside the vast hotel complex of the same name 20km (12½ miles) north of Vilnius on the A2 highway. Spread over 154ha (380 acres) of countryside, the resort is surrounded by fabulous birch forests and beautiful lakes. It focuses on the benefits of aromatherapy and physiotherapy, with treatments that revive, rejuvenate and restore the skin. This is a fairly exclusive resort, with prices to match.
www.lemeridien.lt

Remembering oppression

Located about 125km (78 miles) southwest of Vilnius, just off the main A4 highway to Druskininkai, is a unique sculpture park called Grūto Parkas. Spread over a 20ha (50-acre) area, the park is home to a wealth of Soviet statues taken down from various sites all over the country when Lithuania re-established its independence in 1990. Rather than glorifying the Soviet regime, which was the original purpose of these statues, the park highlights the negative content of Soviet ideology and how it affected the value system of this country.

From 1989 to 1991, during the restoration of independence of the Baltic States, the fate of the Soviet statues was uncertain. Many were dismantled and piled into storehouses and back yards, while others were completely destroyed with dynamite

Stained-glass depiction of Lenin

in neighbouring republics. Viliumas Malinauskas, a local mushroom farmer and entrepreneur, put forward a proposal to the Lithuanian Ministry of Culture that these dismantled sculptures from the Soviet period be displayed in an exhibition. In 1998, his proposal was accepted, and preparatory work began in early 1999. Many of the statues had to be repaired as they were damaged during the rebellion. Many still bear the scars, including splashes of paint and the occasional fissure or dent.

There was much controversy over the opening of the park. Many Lithuanians strongly objected to the exhibition of these sculptures and other ideological relics. For those who had lost their loved ones during the oppressive regime or had suffered in other ways, the idea of having such an exposition, designed along theme-park lines, seemed like a shocking travesty. Arguments in favour of the establishment of the park included the importance of this new tourist sight for southern Lithuania, and the fact that the park would not be a glorification of the former oppressors but rather the opposite. And, indeed, the stated aim of Grūto Parkas is to change the ideological purport of the

Detail of a relief at Grūto Parkas

huge Soviet sculptures by the way they are exhibited. Grūto Parkas was officially opened on 1 April 2001, significantly known in Lithuania as the Day of Liars.

The sculptures on display include several Lenins (featuring one of only three statues of the man ever made of him sitting down), a handful of Stalins, plus Angarietis, Kapsukas, Dzerzhinsky, members of the Youth Communist League, soldiers, writers, workers and other traitors. The display seeks to symbolise the cruelty and absurdity of the Soviet regime. The order in which the monuments are displayed reflects the weight of the role that each of these people (or groups of people) took in the organisation and implementation of terror, and in the annihilation of the sovereignty of Lithuania. Barbed wire fencing, watchtowers and replicas of cattle trucks, such as were used to deport people, all create the impression of a Siberian concentration camp in the middle of a Lithuanian forest.

OTHER GRŪTO PARKAS ATTRACTIONS

As well as the monuments mentioned here, Grūto Parkas also features a wooden information centre built in the style of houses of the 1940s and 1950s, an interesting collection of Soviet art and design, a children's playground made from original Soviet-era swings and roundabouts and a small restaurant serving Soviet-themed dishes.

Grūtas village. Tel: (8-313) 55 511.
Open: 9am–sunset. Admission charge.

Drive: Druskininkai to the Žuvintas Strict State Reserve

This scenic south–north drive provides a few interesting and occasionally poignant diversions, starting at the spa town of Druskininkai and ending in the spectacular area known as the Žuvintas Strict State Reserve. Taking it easy along a few of the country's less used roads, this journey taken during the late summer promises many glimpses into the lives of rural Lithuanian folk. Watch out for horses and carts along the way.

Time: Allow three and a half hours.

Distance: 60km (37 miles).

1 Druskininkai

This interesting spa town (*see pp68–72*) makes for a good start to the drive.

Leave Druskininkai heading northwest on the 180 following the signs for Lazdijai. As the countryside opens up you'll spot large wooden crosses by the side of the road and huge abandoned collective farms from the days of the Soviet occupation.

2 Leipalingis

At Leipalingis follow the 180 north in the direction of Seirijai. Look out on the right for a sign that says Žydų Genocido Kapai. Turn right here for a brief and chilling diversion.

3 Žydų Genocido Kapai (Jewish Genocide Graves)

Just past a sharp left-hand bend in the road by a deserted wooden house, a track on the left of the road to the lakeside resort of Šilaičiai leads to a small clearing in the woods next to a large lake. A small monument stands in the clearing. On it is written: 'In this place was spilled the blood of 953 Jewish children, women and men. They were cruelly killed on 11.9.1941 by the Nazis and their conspirators.'

Turn round and get back onto the main road.

4 Seirijai

Seirijai is a small, good-looking town that was the centre of the German Calvinist movement in Lithuania at the end of the 16th century.

Drive through Seirijai and continue north over the crossroads on the 181 north towards Simnas. (To reach your destination by a more scenic route, a few kilometres before Simnas, soon after a tiny village called Akuočiai, there's a turning off to the left which will bring you to one of the two lakes that flank this stretch of road. Continue into Simnas and head out of town on the 181. A few kilometres after Simnas turn off the main road towards Aleknonys and you'll see the signs for the Žuvintas Strict State Reserve.

5 Žuvintas Strict State Reserve

In the tiny settlement of Aleknonys is the Žuvintas Strict State Reserve Visitors' Centre (*see p73*), easily spotted thanks to a tall statue of a crane on the grass in front of it. Walk down to the lake to its left and you will come across a slatted wooden walkway that leads out into the water. It's quite decrepit, so proceed with caution. The views from here across the deeper part of the lake are lovely on a sunny day. Take a pair of binoculars if you want to do some bird watching.

From here you can head north to the E28 in the direction of Birštonas and Kaunas, both mentioned in this guidebook.

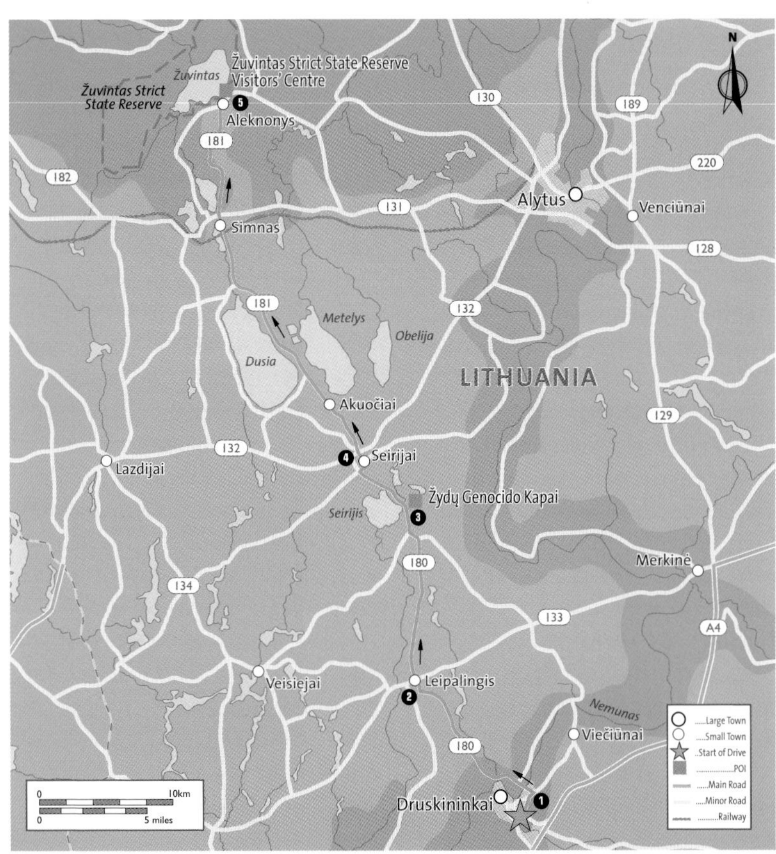

Laisvės Alėja, pedestrianised and lined with trees, stretches for 1.6km (1 mile)

Kaunas

Lithuania's second largest city in terms of population with around 380,000 inhabitants, Kaunas is an attractive place to spend a couple of days or to use as a base while exploring the central part of the country. The old town is full of historic buildings and is a very pleasant place to wander around. Its new town is no less interesting. Kaunas is also the most Lithuanian of Lithuanian towns and cities, claiming a higher percentage of locals than any other place in the country.

Kaunas' geographical location on the confluence of the Neris and Nemunas rivers made it a place of extreme strategic importance in medieval times. As such, it was constantly under attack in the 14th century from the Teutonic Knights. The fortress in Kaunas was successfully breached by the Knights in 1361, and it was at this point that the town first appeared in written texts. It had a period of prosperity and commercial importance after the joint Polish-Lithuanian defeat of the Teutonic Order at the Battle of Žalgiris in 1410, as it was then able to use its excellent strategic location for promoting trade and business rather than for military defence purposes. Records from the 15th and 16th centuries show continued prosperity and consolidation of its position as a vital commercial centre. However, decay began to take hold of the city at the end of the 18th century and the ensuing century of Russian rule kept it very much behind Vilnius, which had managed to negotiate a certain amount of cultural autonomy from the Russian regime.

When Lithuania established its independent statehood after the conflict with Poland between the world wars, Kaunas became the interim capital. With this new identity, it began to flourish. By the beginning of the 1930s, the city was reinventing itself as a capital with elegant architecture and a burgeoning cultural life. Kaunas became, and still is today, an important centre of learning and culture.
Kaunas Tourist Information Centre. Laisvės Alėja 36. Tel: (8-37) 32 34 36. www.visit.kaunas.lt

Laisvės Alėja (Freedom Avenue)
This vast, tree-lined avenue is 1.6km (1 mile) long and contains the city's smartest hotels, trendiest restaurants and bars, and a host of swanky fashion shops. It was once forbidden to smoke on this street, which remains a popular meeting-place for the city's young people who spend hours walking up and down, stopping at the occasional café or just chatting in groups.

Lietuvos Aviacijos Muziejus (Lithuanian Aviation Museum)
This fascinating little museum features a few rooms of treats including none other than a Heath Robinson-style Soviet-built flight simulator. Outside sit scores of planes and helicopters, some of them real beauties and all of them rusting away for lack of funds.
Veiverių 132. Tel. (8-37) 39 03 57. Open: 9am–5pm. Closed: Sun & Mon. Admission charge.

MK Čiurlionio Dailės Muziejus (MK Čiurlionis Art Museum)
Set up after his death when Kaunas was the temporary capital of the country, this museum features both an extensive collection of Čiurlionis' (*see p72*) paintings as well as the opportunity to listen to some of his music.
Putvinskio 55. Tel: (8-37) 22 94 75. Open: 11am–5pm. Closed: Mon. Admission charge.

Mykolo Žilinsko Dailės Galerija (Mykolas Žilinskas Art Gallery)
Just across the square from Šv Arkangelo Mykolo Bažnyčia in the southwest corner is the fine Mykolas Žilinskas Art Museum. On the ground floor is an exhibition of decorative art, with paintings and sculptures displayed on the two upper floors. Outside the

The eternal flame lights up the Freedom Monument in Kaunas

The impressive Church of St Michael the Archangel

museum you cannot fail to see Petras Mazūras's sculpture of a nude man, which caused a certain amount of outrage when it was installed in 1990. The museum is also noteworthy for housing the only Rubens in the country.
Nepriklausomybės Aikštė 12.
Tel: (8-37) 22 28 53. Open: 11am–5pm. Closed: Mon. Admission charge.

Šv Arkangelo Mykolo Bažnyčia (Church of St Michael the Archangel)
This huge neo-Byzantine church at the far eastern end of Laisvės Alėja was built between 1891 and 1893 for Orthodox worship, but finally became a Roman Catholic Church in 1990. It is also known as Soboras, a Lithuanian rendering of the Russian *sobor*, meaning cathedral. Designed and constructed by Russian architects, it was built for the Kaunas Military Garrison. It was converted into an art gallery during the Soviet period and reopened as a place of worship in the early 1990s.
Nepriklausomybės Aikštė.

Velnių Muziejus (Devil Museum)
Established in 1966 in the house of the artist Antanas Žmuidzinavičius (1876–1966), this museum houses major works of the artist as well as his personal collection of artefacts which he bequeathed to the state. The artist was a prolific collector of Lithuanian art, historic and ethnographic objects and folk artefacts. It is also known as the Devil's Museum as it exhibits a collection of over 2,000 devil-related sculptures and works of art from all over the world, including those of Hitler and Stalin depicted as devils, doing the dance of death over a playground called Lithuania, littered with human bones.
Putvinskio 64. Tel: (8-37) 22 15 87. Open: 11am–5pm. Closed: Mon. Admission charge.

Vytauto Didžiojo Karo Muziejus (Vytautas the Great Military Museum)
Huge bronze lions guard the entrance of the Vytautas the Great Military Museum, which was founded in the 1920s to honour the military history of Lithuania. Among the rooms full of militaria, although it has nothing to do

Man by Petras Mazūras stands at the entrance to the Mykolas Žilinskas Art Gallery

with the military, is the wreck of Lithuanian aviators Steponas Darius and Stasys Girėnas' plane, *Lituanica*. These two national heroes, who can be found on the front of the blue 10Lt banknote, were born in Lithuania but grew up in the United States. Their bravery and daring led them to be embraced into Lithuanian historical culture. They plunged to their deaths in 1933 under suspicious circumstances as they were attempting to break the world record for the longest transatlantic flight. There's a 25m (82ft) high bronze memorial statue to the pair on Sporto, next to the football stadium that also bears their name.
Donelaičio 64. Tel: (8-37) 32 09 39. Open: 10am–5pm. Closed: Mon & Tue. Admission charge.

Children playing outside the Vytautas the Great Military Museum

Kėdainiai

Located about 40km (25 miles) north of Kaunas, Kėdainiai offers a convenient stop-off on a tour of the area. The ancient market town is set on the banks of the Nevėžis River and has an attractive and well-preserved old town with a fine main square. In the early 16th century it was owned by the grand Protestant Radvila family who tried to establish the town as an intellectual and cultural centre. Any remaining signs of Protestant culture date from this period. The variety of churches and two synagogues are evidence of the tolerance and inclusiveness that Kėdainiai has shown, embracing Jewish, Russian Orthodox, Arian and Catholic communities over the centuries.
Tourist Information Centre. Didžioji 1. Tel: (8-347) 60 363. www.visitkedainiai.lt

Kėdainių Daugiakultūris Centras (Kėdainiai Multicultural Centre)
What was the smaller of the city's two synagogues is now this hive of activity, featuring a contemporary art gallery among other things. Definitely worth a visit, exhibitions of contemporary art, sculpture and photography are held throughout the year.
Senoji Rinka 12. Tel: (8-347) 51 778. Open: 10am–5pm. Closed: Sun & Mon. Admission charge.

Kėdainių Krašto Muziejus (Kėdainiai Regional Museum)

The museum is housed in an attractive 18th-century former Carmelite convent. There's a substantial number of exhibits relating to the town's most renowned resident, Duke Jonušas Radvila (1612–55), including a number of portraits of different members of his illustrious family. The development of the town is also interestingly presented through the use of models and pictures. One exhibit you must not miss, if only to marvel at the grotesqueness of it, is the room of 19th-century furniture made out of antlers.

Didžioji 19. Tel: (8-347) 53 685. Open: 10am–5pm. Closed: Sun & Mon. Admission charge.

Kėdainiai's synagogues

Reformatų Bažnyčia (Evangelical Reform Church)

This is one of the town's main landmarks and is of interest as a fine example of this type of austere Protestant architecture, but more importantly, in local history terms, for the mausoleum of the Radvila Dukes. Considered the most notable royal grave in Lithuania, the mausoleum is in the basement underneath the main altar. The remains of Jonušas, his grandfather Kristupas 'The Thunderer' and four of Jonušas' siblings are laid out in wonderfully ornate Baroque coffins of varying sizes. The largest and grandest belongs to Jonušas, and the four small coffins on little brass legs belong to his infant siblings. Contact the Tourist Information Centre (*see p84*) to organise a visit to the church and/or the mausoleum.

Senoji 1.

JEWISH KĖDAINIAI

The existence of a once substantial Jewish community in Kėdainiai is evidenced by the two remaining synagogues in the old town. Jews were first recorded as living in the city in the 15th century but were banished at the end of the century by Archduke Alexander. It wasn't until the mid-17th century that the Jewish community was properly established and then, as licensors for the production of beer and spirits, they became the hostelry owners and the social and economic backbone of the population. Since the devastation of the Jewish community here during World War II, little of their cultural heritage remains, except for the two synagogues, of which the larger of the two now operates as an art school.

Walk: Kaunas old town

Boasting majestic buildings and fine stonework, Kaunas' old town is a wonderful place to wander around. This walk begins in the 13th-century main street, Vilniaus, and takes you around the main sights of the old town up to Kaunas Castle, down to the river and back to the main street.

Time: Allow two or three hours.

Distance: 2.5km (1½ miles).

Begin the walk at St Peter and St Paul's Cathedral.

1 Šv Petro ir Pauliaus Arkikatedra (St Peter and St Paul's Cathedral)

Dating from 1408, with minor Renaissance and Baroque flourishes added in the 17th century, this spectacular church is the only Gothic church in Lithuania with a basilica floor-plan. It is the final resting place of the Lithuanian priest and poet Maironis (1862–1932) and Bishop Motiejus Valančius (1801–75), whose illegal printing and distributing of Lithuanian literature under Tsarist rule has won him an eternal place in the nation's heart.
Head north up Valančiaus and take the second left into Pilies. Continue down Pilies across Jakšto to reach Kaunas Castle.

2 Kauno Pilis (Kaunas Castle)

The oldest building in the city, Kaunas Castle had been in existence years before it was first chronicled in 1361.
Walk around the building and into the park, coming back onto Papilio.

3 Šv Jurgio Bažnyčia ir Vienuolynas (St George's Church and Monastery)

This friary was built for the Bernardine Order in Gothic style in the 15th century. Its condition deteriorated greatly during the Soviet regime and it is currently under restoration.
Continue along Papilio, turning right into Jakšto and right when you reach Town Hall Square (Rotušės Aikštė).

4 Šv Trejybės Bažnyčia (St Trinity Church)

Now used as a dance studio, the exterior features a mixture of Renaissance and Gothic architecture.
Walk back into the main square.

5 Rotušė (Town Hall)

Kaunas' Town Hall dates from the mid-16th century and is predominantly late

Baroque in style. It is best remembered as a Soviet wedding palace and nicknamed 'White Swan'.

Turn left down Mutinės.

6 Šv Pranciškaus Ksavero Jėzuitų Bažnyčia (St Francis Xavier Jesuit Church)

Built in 1666, the church was converted to Russian Orthodox use in 1825 and raised to cathedral status in 1843. Used as a school during the Soviet era, it has been back in Catholic service since 1990.

Turn right down Aleksoto.

7 Perkūno Namas (Thunder House)

Built at the end of the 15th century, this building with its classic Gothic gable has been under the control of Jesuits and tradesmen at various points in its history. It plays host to art classes.

Walk on down Aleksoto until you reach the river. Turn left.

8 Vytauto Didžiojo Bažnyčia (Church of Vytautas the Great)

This once glorious church was built by Franciscan monks at the start of the 15th century, used as an ammunition warehouse by the Napoleonic army and was an Orthodox cathedral under the Tsarist occupation. It's now back safely in Catholic hands.

Walk along the river on Karaliaus Mindaugo. Turn left up Daukšos and right into Kurpių. Continue along here and turn left at Palangos and take the first right into Vilniaus.

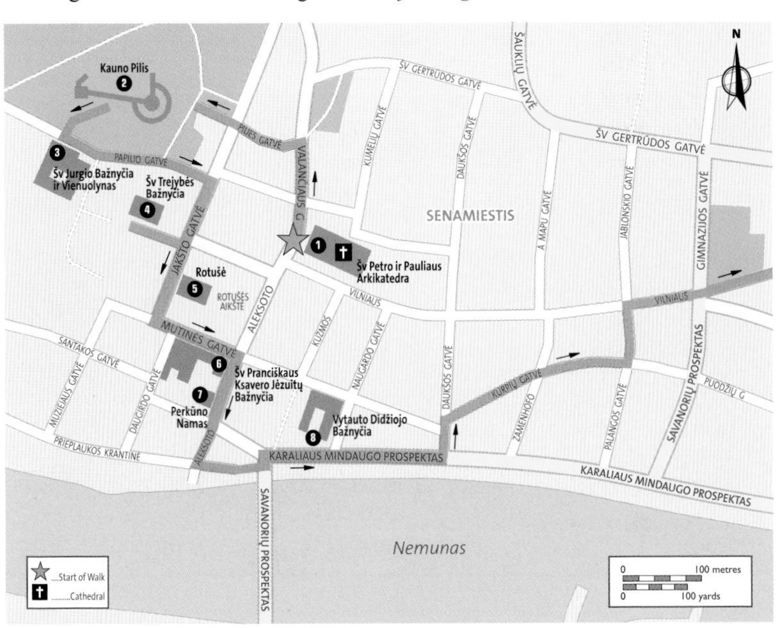

The Baltic coast

Lithuania's Baltic coast offers a variety of attractions. The pièce de résistance *is the Kuršių Nerija, or Curonian Spit. One of the country's designated national parks, it was recognised by UNESCO in 2000 as a World Heritage Site. Stretching 97km (60 miles) in length, of which some 50km (32 miles) is in Lithuania, and only 4km (2½ miles) across at its widest part, this thin strip of sand consists mainly of forests and dunes and protects a huge inland body of water, the Curonian Lagoon, and the mainland from the mighty Baltic Sea. It is almost without doubt the most beautiful, unspoilt and peaceful area in the country.*

The Curonian Spit is accessible from the mainland by ferries that run from two small ports in Klaipėda, Lithuania's third largest city. About 30km (19 miles) along the coast north of Klaipėda is the country's summer capital, Palanga, a lively and attractive place immensely popular with Lithuanians and a growing number of foreign tourists both as a peaceful health resort out of season and as the country's main seaside destination for

Sunset over the Baltic Sea

party animals during the short summer season between June and September. Booking a room here during hot weekends can be problematic, and booking in advance is highly recommended.

Klaipėda

With over 203,000 inhabitants, Klaipėda is the third largest city in the country population-wise. In terms of commercial and strategic importance and cosmopolitan appeal, Klaipėda could be rated as Lithuania's second city rather than Kaunas, which has a larger population.

Built around Lithuania's only sea port, Klaipėda and its two satellite holiday resorts, Nida to the south and Palanga to the north, are well on their way to collectively becoming a Baltic Riviera. In summer, the city itself is

The Baltic coast

German influence on the architecture is evident in these buildings in Klaipėda

usually not the main attraction, with most tourists heading towards the beach resorts nearby. But with its museums, monuments, galleries and historic buildings, it's got plenty to occupy those interested in some sightseeing and culture.

Klaipėda has been part of Lithuania only since 1923 when it was seized by the inter-war republic. For most of its previous life it had existed as the German city of Memel, and was the easternmost outpost of the Second Reich. Once you're aware of its history, the architecture prevalent in the older part of town begins to make sense. There are some lovely buildings here, but they are surprisingly different from the architecture in the other Lithuanian cities. The rest of the city has changed completely, as has the population, consisting mainly of Lithuanians, although a sizeable ethnic Russian population who settled here after World War II still exists. The German population has all but disappeared.

Like Vilnius and Kaunas, Klaipėda also has two distinct parts. The old town, where most of the museums are located, is to the south of the Danė River, which cuts the city in two. The new town sits immediately over the water on the Danė's northern shore.

When you've had enough of sightseeing in the city and fancy a break, head north out of Klaipėda either on foot, bicycle or bus towards

Palanga and you soon reach the beautiful sandy beaches of Melnragė and then a bit further on to Giruliai. There are many outdoor restaurants, cafés and bars lining the beaches, and a smattering of water sports is available. Just across the lagoon to the southwest of the city, Smiltynė is a popular beach area reached by a short ferry ride from Klaipėda.
Tourist Information Centre. Turgaus 7. Tel: (8-46) 41 21 86. www.klaipeda.lt

Centrinis Paštas (Central Post Office)

Don't miss this truly outstanding building. A wonderful example of German neo-Gothic architecture, this red brick mansion was designed by the architect H Schode in 1893 and is a beautiful building both inside and out (there are few better and more charming places in the world in which to post a letter). Alongside is a lofty, 44m (144ft) bell tower that houses the largest musical instrument in the country. Built in Apolde in Germany, the immense 48-bell carillon is rung at noon on weekends. Concerts are also organised at times.
Liepų 16. Open: 8am–6pm. Closed: Sat & Sun.

Kalvystės Muziejus (Blacksmith's Museum)

A few minutes' walk from Theatre Square, the focal point of the old town, leads visitors to this excellent interactive museum. Watch the action at a real working forge manned by hardworking blacksmiths. Also included are a number of interesting metalwork exhibits such as church weather vanes and metal crosses.
Saltkalvių 2. Tel: (8-46) 41 05 26. Open: 10am–5.30pm. Closed: Sun & Mon. Admission charge.

Laikrodžių Muziejus (Timepiece Museum)

An unusual and interesting museum is the city's Timepiece Museum. It contains timepieces from the earliest days – including candles and ingenious water clocks – to the latest gadgets of the present. As with many of the country's museums, a lack of descriptions makes the museum a little baffling at times but is still worth a visit all the same, if only for the novelty value.

KGB MEMORIALIN KAMERA (KGB MEMORIAL ROOM)

A small plaque on the wall of Klaipėda's former KGB headquarters, now the main administrative building for the city's branch of the Lithuanian Customs department, marks the space above a tiny 12sq m (130sq ft) room in the building's basement where people arrested by the KGB were held. Unlike its much larger counterpart in Vilnius, the so-called Memorial Room is yet to operate as a fully functioning museum, and at the time of writing little information about what went on in the room and the building in general is available to the public. Holding just a bed, the room serves as a poignant reminder of Lithuania's Soviet occupation. To see it, call the number below to arrange an appointment.
Neries 4. Tel: (8-46) 39 01 09.

A Soviet-era statue in Klaipėda

Liepų 12. Tel: (8-46) 41 04 13. Open: noon–5.30pm, Sun noon–4.30pm. Closed: Mon. Admission charge.

Lietuvos Jūrų Muziejus (Lithuanian Sea Museum)
The only attraction of its kind in the Baltic States, Klaipėda's superb Sea Museum contains both a dolphinarium, with the usual shows for adults and children alike, as well as an aquarium containing a wealth of aquatic life. Sea lion shows and other antics also take place here during the summer. Find it over the water on the northern tip of the Curonian Lagoon. To get there take a ferry from the Old Castle and head to the right along the water's edge.
Smiltynės 3. Tel: (8-46) 49 07 51. Open: 10.30am–6pm. Closed: Mon & Tue.

Mažosios Lietuvos Istorijos Muziejus (Lithuania Minor History Museum)
It's worth stopping off at this old town attraction to get some sense of the history of the city and its surrounding area. The collection is eclectic and interesting and just being inside the building is an experience in itself, the interior resembling the inside of a wooden sailing ship.
Didžioji Vandens 6. Tel: (8-46) 41 05 24. Open: 10am–6pm. Closed: Sun & Mon. Admission charge.

Half-timbered building in Klaipėda old town

Teatro Aikštė (Theatre Square)

The centre of the city's diminutive old town, Theatre Square is dominated by the 19th-century **Klaipėdos Dramos Teatras (Klaipėda Drama Theatre)**, the venue for many significant cultural and political events including Adolf Hitler's announcement of Klaipėda's reincorporation into Germany from the building's exterior balcony in 1939. Wagner also once performed here as a visiting conductor. The statue of Annchen von Tarau erected in 1912 (*see box*) in front of the Drama Theatre is dedicated to the 17th-century German poet Simon Dach.

This square, although really quite charming, remains a little bleak, with only one restaurant with outside tables on it.

ANNCHEN VON TARAU (TARAVOS ANIKĖ)

The statue of the girl standing with her back to the Klaipėda Drama Theatre in the centre of Teatro Aikštė was dedicated to the German poet Simon Dach (1605–59), who wrote a famous folk song about the girl. The story of the girl is a bit of a mystery. All that's known is that the statue of her disappeared some time during World War II. She was either abducted by the Soviets or the Nazis, the latter possibly being upset that her back was turned towards Hitler when he addressed the masses from the theatre's balcony, and the former simply because of their infamous propensity for destruction at the time. The current statue is a replica made in 1989 from photographs of the original.

Palanga

Lithuania's premier fun seaside resort, Palanga combines the bustle of a hectic holiday destination with a number of

Annchen von Tarau and the Drama Theatre

Notice some of the interesting features on Klaipėda's older buildings

nearby places to get away from it all. On offer are long, pale sandy beaches backed by dunes, excellent swimming, a large botanical garden and a vibrant town with modern facilities. Palanga's resident population of around 20,000 swells to over 100,000 between June and August, when Lithuanians from all over the country and tourists from countries as far away as Russia and the UK descend upon it in droves. It's hard to imagine now that the town was once a fishing village and later Lithuania's main port from the 15th to the 17th century. Its popularity as a resort and health spa grew in the 19th century when Count Felix Tiškevičius bought a large estate on the outskirts of the town and built a huge mansion and park. This inspired others to set up guesthouses, and by the beginning of the 20th century Palanga had become a fashionable health resort, favoured by the aristocracy of Lithuania, Poland and Russia.

Tourist Information Centre. Kretingos 1. Tel: (8-460) 48 811. www.palangatic.lt

Gintaro Muziejus (Amber Museum)

The fine neo-Classical mansion that houses this excellent museum was built at the end of the 19th century for Count Tiškevičius' family. The museum showcases the interesting history of this semi-precious Baltic Gold, and displays hundreds of interesting pieces of the stuff. Concerts and recitals are also held here throughout the year.

Botanical Park. Tel: (8-460) 53 501. Open: 10am–8pm, Sun 10am–7pm. Closed: Mon. Admission charge.

Walk: Palanga

The most interesting parts of Palanga cover a relatively small area. This route covers them in some detail, and is full of opportunities to relax along the way.

Time: Allow about two hours, depending on how long you want to spend in the Botanical Park.

Distance: 3km (2 miles).

Start the walk at the Tourist Information Centre next to the bus station close to the intersection of Kretingos and Vytauto.

1 Šv Mergelės Marijos Ėmimo į Dangų Bažnyčia (Holy Virgin Mary Ascension Church)

This imposing red brick neo-Gothic church at the junction of Kretingos and Vytauto was built between 1897 and 1906 to the plans of the Swedish architect K Strandman. The 76m (250ft) spire is one of the symbols of the city. On the opposite side of the road is a large Soviet-era monument dedicated to those who lost their lives during World War II.

Continue along Vytauto over the small Rąžė River until you reach the sculpture park on your right.

2 Sculpture park

Set up by the Lithuanian National Art Museum Fund, this small grassy space features a dozen or so small sculptures from Lithuanian artists including Nijolė Gaigalaitė and Dailutė Matulaitė.

Keep heading south until you get to the Palanga Botanical Park.

3 Palangos Botanikos Parkas (Palanga Botanical Park)

Designed by the renowned French landscape architect Édouard André (1867–1942), this park was commissioned by Count Felix Tiškevičius in 1897. Covering an area of 100ha (247 acres), it's one of the most beautiful and best-preserved parks in Lithuania.

4 Eglė Žalčių Karalienė (Eglė Queen of Serpents Statue)

Sculpted by Robertas Antinis, this statue between the northeastern entrance to the park and the Amber Museum depicts the moment when the heroine of the story finds a snake in her blouse (*see pp98–9*).

5 Gintaro Muziejus (Amber Museum)

For details see p95.

Keep walking around the right-hand side of the museum until you reach a point where the path splits. Both ways lead in the direction of the next sight, the right-hand way taking you out of the park and along Mielės.

6 Tiltas (Pier)

Originally a 19th-century landing stage, Palanga's current 470m (1,540ft) pier dates from 1997 and is a hugely popular place for strolling and for gathering to watch the sun set.

Head east to the start of Basanavičiaus.

7 Basanavičiaus

Named after one of the founding fathers of the modern Lithuanian state, Basanavičiaus runs east–west for almost a kilometre. Now entirely pedestrianised, the street is packed with bars, restaurants and amusement parks.

Walk down to the end of Basanavičiaus to where it intersects Vytauto, the road where the walk began.

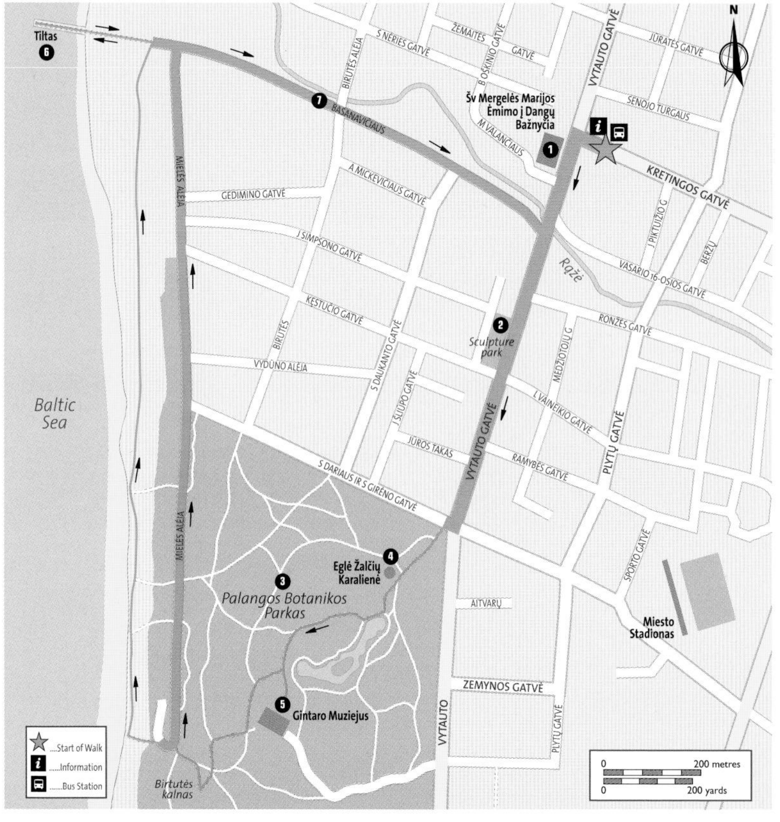

Eglė, Queen of Serpents

A long time ago, according to one of Lithuania's best-known legends, Eglė, Queen of Serpents (Eglė Žalčių Karalienė), there lived an old man and his wife, who had twelve sons and three daughters. One hot summer's day, the three sisters decided to go for a dip in a lake to cool off. After their swim, they climbed back onto the riverbank to put on their clothes. To her distress, Eglė, the youngest of the three girls, found a snake inside her blouse.

The eldest sister attempted to scare off the snake by shaking the blouse and jumping on it, but to no avail. The snake would not be intimidated. Instead, it turned to Eglė and spoke in a man's voice, asking for her hand in marriage in return for not harming her or her sisters. Feeling she had no choice, Eglė agreed to the contract, through a mist of tears.

When the girls came back to their home, which they shared with their parents and twelve brothers, hundreds of snakes surrounded the house demanding that Eglė return with them to the lake to fulfil her promise. Eglė's father, who was desperate not to lose his youngest and most beautiful daughter, tried to trick the snakes by sending different animals dressed as Eglė to accompany the snakes back to the lake. The serpents soon saw through each of these deceptions, which did nothing but anger them further, and they returned to the farm demanding the bride. Eventually Eglė's father had no choice but to give up his daughter. Reluctantly, Eglė left her home. To her surprise, she was greeted by a handsome prince who was waiting for her by the beach. The prince told her how much he had enjoyed watching her swim. Needless to say, Eglė instantly fell in love with the prince and they were married, and soon had children, three sons and a daughter. Eglė was so happy that she quickly forgot her homeland. They lived together happily in the lake for many years until fate took an unexpected and dark turn for them.

One day, Eglė's three sons asked if they could meet their grandparents. It was only at this point that Eglė remembered her old home and naturally she agreed to take them to visit her family. However, while visiting the family, Eglė's daughter was tricked by Eglė's brothers into revealing how to call forth the prince from the lake. The brothers took off to the lakeside with this information and called Eglė's

Eglė shaking the serpent out of her blouse

husband from the waters. When he swam up, the brothers chopped him to pieces. They then returned to the farm, not breathing a word of their deed to Eglė.

Nine days passed, and Eglė returned to the lake to be united with her husband. When she called for him she was greeted by foam and blood, and she heard the voice of her beloved husband, telling her what her brothers had done. Heartbroken, Eglė in utter despair turned herself and her children into trees. She herself became a fir tree. She changed her three sons into the strongest of the trees, oak, ash and birch. And she turned her daughter into the quivering weeping willow, for she had quavered under pressure from her uncles and had betrayed her father.

Kuršių Nerija (The Curonian Spit)

A unique, quite wonderful piece of land, the Curonian Spit is a thin peninsula of sand covered by forests and dunes that protects the huge inland body of water to its east called the Curonian Lagoon (Kuršių Marios), as well as the mainland, from the rigours of the Baltic Sea. The spit covers a length of 97km (60 miles), but only a stretch of 52km (32 miles) belongs to Lithuania, the remainder in the south being part of the Russian oblast of Kaliningrad.

Extending from the Semba Peninsula in the south to the Strait of Klaipėda in the north, the spit is 4km (2½ miles) across at its widest point, and, at the narrowest point, the Baltic Sea is separated from the Curonian Lagoon by only 400m (1,310ft).

The Curonian Spit was created more than 5,000 years ago by the waves and winds of the Baltic Sea. The spit's formation began when a barren strip of sand separated the Curonian Lagoon from the Baltic Sea. Over the passage of time, the sand gradually shifted

Dunes and beach on the Curonian Spit

The calm inshore waters of the Curonian Lagoon, Neringa

eastwards and was deposited in the lagoon, thus forming the Curonian Spit. Its eastern shore is on the Curonian Lagoon, while the western shore of the peninsula is met by the Baltic Sea. A UNESCO-protected World Heritage Site since 2000, the spit and its native flora and fauna are protected by strict guidelines set by the Lithuanian authorities. Half of the territory on the Lithuanian end has been assigned to reserve. One fifth is designated for recreational use.

Around 72 per cent of the Curonian Spit is covered by forests. The fact that such large forest cover of mostly conifers and grasslands is possible on the sandy soil of the spit is remarkable in itself. Several unusual species of flora are found here. Sand dunes occupy 12 per cent of the area. The spit's unique landscape of high and bare sand dunes alternating with forest harbours a variety of wildlife, especially birdlife. Its position makes it an important spot for studying routes taken by migratory birds.

From the top of the high sand dunes you get an unforgettable view. On one side are the rolling waves of the Baltic Sea and, on the other, the waters of the Curonian Lagoon. Between these two bodies of water, a strip of sand stretches into the distance, with glades, sparse settlements, lighthouses and forests.

Getting there

The Lithuanian part of the spit can only be reached by ferry; it is connected to land at the Russian end. Unfortunately, there is still plenty of red tape at the

Russian border, preventing easy trips to this part of the spit. There are two ferry services from Klaipėda to the spit, running at regular intervals and both allowing foot passengers, cars and bicycles on board. Regular minibuses meet the northern (Old Castle) ferry and run up and down the entire length of the spit. The 50km (31-mile) journey from top to bottom still costs less than 10Lt. Having your own car gives you the freedom to explore at leisure as well as undertake the road trip described in this guide (*see pp106–7*). Once you arrive on the spit, if you haven't brought a vehicle, flag down any of the minibuses to get to the main beaches. The permit needed to travel to the municipality of Neringa is available for purchase when you arrive at its border. No permit is required to visit the northern beach towns such as Kopgalis or Smiltynė.

One of the many art pieces on display in Neringa

Neringa

The longest town in Lithuania at 50km (31 miles), Neringa's population now stands at 2,700. It was formed in 1961 when the separate villages of Nida, Preila, Pervalka and Juodkrantė were joined to form a single administrative unit.

There's plenty to do even for those not interested in swimming or sunbathing on the spit's pristine beaches. The lagoon is a great place to fish, row or sail. Visitors can also explore the berry- and mushroom-rich forests, which play a vital role in protecting the villages from the shifting sands. Picking mushrooms is a national pastime, and wherever you go in Lithuania in season, you're likely to see people out with buckets, scouring the ground for these tasty delicacies. In the morning you can look on the beach for pieces of amber, as the sea sometimes washes handfuls of pieces ashore, especially after a good storm.

The architecture here is particularly interesting. Nowhere else in Lithuania will you see so many colourfully decorated houses. Bright weather vanes stand out on the roofs of the houses along the spit; now, as in the past, it's important for a fisherman to know which way the wind's blowing. Fishing is not simply an occupation on the Curonian Spit, it's a way of life, and the evening air often smells of smoked fish.

Nida

The biggest settlement and the most popular destination on the spit is Nida at the far southern end of the Lithuania section of the spit. It can be a bit overcrowded in the peak season, attracting over 50,000 tourists per year. Nida is surrounded by pine groves, and is fabulous in winter when the lagoon freezes over. It's a good idea to go at that time if you are looking for some peace and quiet in lovely surroundings, and a host of museums awaits the culture aficionado.

Two aspects of this resort, and for some the main draws, are its dunes and the beach. Not far south of the village, approached from the village itself, is a path that leads to wooden steps that climb to the top of Parnidžio Kopa (Parnidis Dune). At 50m (164ft) high, it's one of the largest dunes on the spit, with great views from its summit. The beach, a fantastic stretch of pale sand, can be reached by walking westwards from here or from the village.

Evangelikų-Liuteronų Bažnyčia (Evangelical-Lutheran Church)

Built in 1888, this redbrick neo-Gothic church is renowned for its *krikštai*, which are a way of marking and protecting the different graves. The shape and size of the *krikštai* indicate the age and sex of the deceased. Classical concerts are held inside the church during the summer.
Pamario 43.

Gintaro Galerija (Amber Gallery)

This collection of unique objects was collected piece by piece in Juodkrantė and Nida for over 20 years. The biggest lump of amber weighs more than 3kg (6.6lb). There are also other valuable pieces weighing up to half that. The gallery features amber in all its colours and forms as well as some unique pieces of restored antique jewellery and some created by Lithuanian artists.
Pamario 20. Tel: (8-469) 52 573.
Open: 9am–9pm. Admission charge.

Kuršių Nerijos Gyventojų Verslų Ekspozicija (Curonian Spit Livelihood Exhibition)

To learn more about the fishermen's way of life, a visit to the Kuršių Nerijos Gyventojų Verslų Ekspozicija is a must. Scale models of the various types of fishing craft and other aquatic vehicles can be examined, plus there are examples and information on the weather vanes that are peculiar to the fishing fleet of the Curonian Spit. You can also learn about the practices and history of the trade from the photographs and commentary on display.
Kuverto 2. Tel: (8-469) 52 372.
Open: 11am–7pm. Closed: Mon.
Admission charge.

Marijos, Krikščionių Pagalbos Bažnyčia (Mary the Guardian of Christians Catholic Church)

This rather unusual and extremely modern church features a gorgeous

The Thomas Mann House in Nida

reed roof and positively dominates Nida's skyline. It also houses a small art gallery.
Taikos 10. Tel: (8-469) 52 132.

Neringos Istorijos Muziejus (Neringa Historical Museum)
Housed in a modern building, this fascinating little museum looks at the traditional trades, culture and lifestyles of the inhabitants of the Curonian Spit. Including everything from fishing and crow hunting, also on display is the equipment belonging to these occupations, such as fishing tackle, a range of model boats, like the *kurėnas* (a small traditional Curonian boat), and the nets that were used to trap crows. Other galleries contain discoveries from the Stone Age found south of Nida. One section is dedicated to the noble family of the Froeses who lived in Nida for several centuries.
Pamario 53. Tel: (8-469) 51 162. Open: 10am–6pm. Admission charge.

Tomo Mano Namelis (Thomas Mann House)
The renowned German writer and Nobel Prize winner Thomas Mann visited Nida in 1929 when it was still part of Prussia and known as Nidden. He was so enamoured with the place that he decided to build his own charming, thatched summer cottage here, now a museum dedicated to the writer and his family. It's really a museum for Mann enthusiasts and has

photographs of his family, letters and editions of his books.

Skruzdynės 17. Tel: (8-469) 52 260. Open: 10am–6pm. Admission charge.

Žvejo Etnografinė Sodyba (Fishermen's Ethnographic Homestead)

Close to the main square down some of the small narrow streets you can see rows of the immaculate, brightly painted, thatched, traditional fishermen's houses for which Nida is famous. If you want to get a literal inside look at the domestic life of the Curonian fishermen, the place to go is the Žvejo Etnografinė Sodyba, an immaculately decorated reconstruction of a traditional fisherman's house.

Naglių 4. Tel: (8-469) 52 372. Open: 10am–6pm. Admission charge.

BOAT CRUISES ON THE LAGOON

The local cruise company Jukunda offers day-trips around the Curonian Lagoon on their lovely cruise ship *Mecklenburg*. Running from the end of May until the beginning of October, this is a beautiful way to view the natural wonder of the spit. The ship leaves the Klaipėda cruise ships' terminal at 10am, returning at 9pm every Friday, Saturday and Sunday, visiting Juodkrantė along the way. The tour usually makes a three-hour stop in Nida. Food and drink are available on board, and prices remain ludicrously cheap.

www.jukunda.lt

A typical Lithuanian sunset on the Curonian Spit

Drive: Curonian Spit

This exhilarating and scenic drive along the spectacular natural formation that is the Curonian Spit takes in rustic villages, old woods, a refreshing seascape and a number of interesting museums.

Time: Allow three to four hours.

Distance: 50km (31 miles).

Catch the Old Castle ferry on Klaipėda's Žvejų across the water to Smiltynė in the morning. Boats leave at regular intervals. On arrival, head for the introductory pathway by the old woods of the Curonian Spit.

1 Introductory pathway

The pathway, which is 1.6km (1 mile) long and starts at the point where the Old Castle ferry disembarks, has stands that provide descriptions, pictures and drawings of the plants that grow in the area. The easy walk is a good introduction to the natural life of the spit.

Back in your car, head south when finished here, towards Neringa. The permit to visit the town of Neringa can be bought from a kiosk at the entrance to the area.

2 Juodkrantė

The first village, Juodkrantė, is 19km (12 miles) south of Klaipėda on the lagoon side of the spit. It's the second biggest settlement on Neringa, after Nida. The beach was awarded a blue flag in 2004 for the good quality of the lagoon water. Take some time to have a look around this quaint village. The main focus of the village is a promenade along the lagoon with many points of tourist interest along the way. There are a few boats moored here, and generally it's a quiet and restful place. There are a few small grocery shops, and a number of houses sell smoked fish from their converted porches.

Make a stop at the Witches' Hill exposition of wooden outdoor sculptures. During 1979 and 1980, folk artists gathered here to create the 70-odd large wooden sculptures you can see today. Another attraction of the area is one of Lithuania's oldest colonies of grey egrets and big cormorants, just outside Juodkrantė. The village also has a number of hotels and guesthouses and offers a slightly cheaper and less frenetic base for a stay on the spit.

3 Pervalka

This is the smallest of the settlements on Neringa. Bordered by a range of dunes to the west, it's 34km (21 miles) south of Klaipėda. Stop off here briefly if you wish to look around the small souvenir shops or buy some smoked fish.

4 Preila

Located on a bay between Preilos Ragas and Ožkų Ragas, 39km (24 miles) from Klaipėda and overlooking the lagoon, this settlement offers magnificent views across the water. The dunes here are covered with grass and other foliage. The settlement is small but cosy, making it a good retreat destination and is the most popular destination for locals looking for the most relaxing place to stay in the area.

5 Nida

The largest settlement on the spit is the town of Nida (*see pp103–5*), the administrative centre of Neringa. The beach was awarded a blue flag for quality in 2001. It's a good place to stop by for a picnic and a swim. Rest here for a few hours before making your return journey. You can also visit the many museums here. Alternatively, you could stop here for a day or two for a fabulous break away from it all (*see p103*).

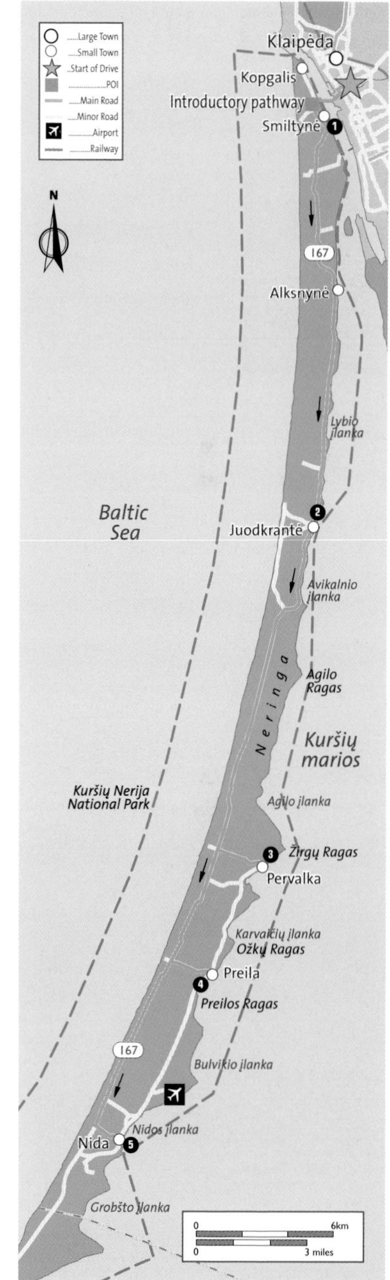

Northern Lithuania

Northern Lithuania is predominantly agricultural but also has a number of interesting nature reserves, regional parks, a couple of relatively large cities and a host of attractive towns and villages. Northern Lithuania has much to offer, including the fact that it's less popular with tourists and thus provides a refreshingly original experience. Šiauliai, the country's fourth biggest city, is a popular base for visiting one of Lithuania's most extraordinary sights, the Hill of Crosses.

Kryžių Kalnas (Hill of Crosses)

Not to be confused with the Hill of Three Crosses in Vilnius (*see p49*), this truly extraordinary sight of literally millions of crosses on a small hill some 12km (7½ miles) north of Šiauliai is

Northern Lithuania

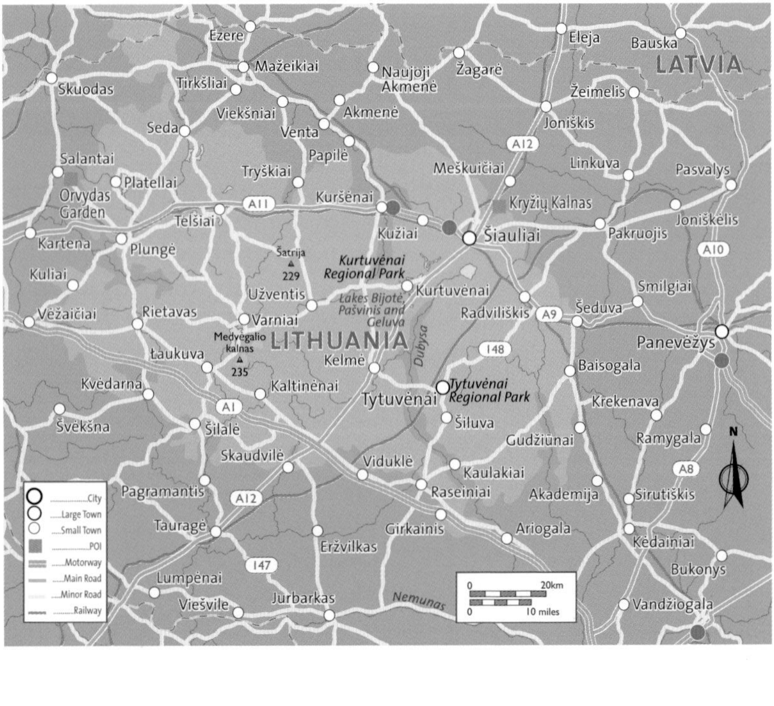

one of Lithuania's most popular destinations. A symbol of Lithuania's history of suffering and of the people's inextinguishable faith, the Hill of Crosses is an essential part of any trip to the region.

The history

Also sometimes referred to as the Hill of Prayers (*Maldų Kalnas*), the Hill of Crosses was originally known as the Jurgaičiai, or Domantai Mound. It was first mentioned as an archaeological monument in the Register of Lithuanian Cultural Heritage at the end of the 19th century, but the mound is thought to have been inhabited since the first millennium. A wooden castle stood on it between the 11th and 14th centuries, but this was burnt down in an assault on the community by the Livonian Order in 1348 and never rebuilt.

The legends

A number of legends have sprung up to explain why the first cross was put up on the mound. One legend tells of an unhappy father whose beloved daughter was dying. He had been visited in a dream by a woman who told him to make a cross and bring it to the hill by the village of Meškuičiai. The father did as he was told, and carried his cross to the hill. It took him 13 hours to get there, and when he returned he was greeted by his daughter, who had miraculously recovered. Once word of the miracle spread, people started bringing their own crosses to the hill. Another version of this legend says that it was a sick man who had simply made a promise to place a cross on the mound if he recovered his health. Another legend says that a manifestation of the Virgin Mary encouraged people to place crosses on the hill.

Whatever the true origin of the legends, the first written record of the site dates from 1850, not long after the 1831 rebellion against the Russians, when many Lithuanians were killed. Their burial places were unknown and it may be that relatives planted the crosses in memory of loved ones who had died during the conflict. After the rebellion of 1863, the numbers increased further.

Every cross has a story attached to it

The Soviets

The Hill of Crosses began to gain a particular significance during the Soviet period as a symbol of resistance to the occupation. After the death of Stalin in the mid-1950s, Lithuanians started returning home from deportations and with them a whole new wave of crosses with inscriptions and stories telling of great suffering

The huge wooden figure of Christ welcomes all who come to pay tribute at the Hill of Crosses

and losses. Lithuania's history was literally being chronicled by the crosses. By 1961, there were over 5,000 crosses and the Soviet government decided things had gone far enough. In an attempt to halt the flow of crosses and do away with the site, the authorities burnt the wooden crosses, destroyed the metal ones, broke up the ones made of stone and threw them into the river. The hill was then flattened with bulldozers and rumours of disease were circulated to justify banning people from the area. The place was put under guard, but still crosses continued to be brought in at night. Known as Bulldozer Atheism, this pattern continued for nearly 20 years. Despite the destructions, believers continued to visit the hill and even organised pious processions, which were strictly forbidden.

The triumph

Once the revival of Lithuanian independence had begun in 1988, the future of the hill was assured and the Hill of Crosses became a permanent feature in the Christian world. The late Pope John Paul II held a mass at the hill in September 1993, ensuring the sacred site's rise to international fame. Its appeal was further enhanced in 1994, when a magnificent crucifix, a present from the Pope, was erected on a mound beside the site to commemorate his visit. Church festivals on the hill have been revived at the foot of this holy gift and the Church Festival of the Holy Cross is held annually during the last weekend of July. The latest addition to this site is a Franciscan monastery built just up the road from the Hill of Crosses in 2000.

Since independence in 1991, the hill has become a monument to the country's defiance and perseverance and a symbol of the suffering caused to so many during the years of occupation.

Visiting the hill today is an extraordinary experience. In some senses it's an eerie place but in another sense it is a celebration. Although your expectation is of a high hill covered with crosses, that's not in fact what the Hill of Crosses is. It is actually a mounded area, not particularly huge and not particularly high. The dramatic effect of the experience comes from the density of the crosses of every imaginable shape and size. There are tiny haphazard paths threading in and out of the crosses that weave over and around the two mounds. The occasional solitary cross looks as though it may be trying to make a run for it, but for the most part they are stacked up against each other with their different shapes, sizes and materials, and even hung with smaller versions of themselves. Rosary beads, together with messages and photographs that hang from some of the crosses, add to the intensity and could be claustrophobic to people with that tendency. The beleaguered wooden Christ near the entrance to the first mound looks as though he is about to fall forward with the weight of all that

Mute swans in Kurtuvėnai

hangs off him. But every cross has a story and a life attached to it, some happy, most sad.

If you visit on a bright sunny day there is a wonder about the place; if you visit on a dark, windy day you will probably feel a pervading stalwart bleakness. All visitors are encouraged to place a cross on the hill and say a prayer before they leave.

Getting there

To get to the Hill of Crosses from Šiauliai, drive north through and out of the city on Tilžės. After about 10km (6¼ miles), close to the village of Jurgaičiai, turn right at the signpost for Kryžių Kalnas. Drive down here a further 2km (1¼ miles). The Hill of Crosses is on your right, and very hard to miss. There are no direct buses to the sight.

Kurtuvėnai Regional Park

Barely ten minutes southwest of Šiauliai, Kurtuvėnai Regional Park makes for a nice and relaxing afternoon trip. A hilly region, the park features a mix of lake and forest landscapes. There's a number of outdoor activities on offer for the more energetic, the most popular being horse riding. The **Kurtuvėnai Riding Stables** (*tel: (8-682) 30 745*) organise horse riding as well as cycling trips, educational journeys, riding courses and recreational events. You can also hire bikes and skis here and there's a small hotel if you want to spend the night. Other overnight options are the campsites by the lakes Bijotė, Pašvinis and Geluva, and by the Dubysa River. It's also a good fishing spot.
Kurtuvėnai Regional Park. Parko 2, Kurtuvėnai. Tel: (8-41) 37 03 36. www.kurtuva.lt

Panevėžys

Lithuania's fifth largest city with a population of around 130,000, Panevėžys straddles both banks of the Nevėžis River from whence the town gets its name. Not the most obvious tourist destination, Panevėžys does, if you dig deep enough, possess its own charm and style, and is worthy of a short visit for those with the time on their hands who are looking for a more authentic Lithuanian experience.

Although a settlement has existed here since the 15th century, it wasn't until the industrial revolution that Panevėžys really got going. Notable for an abundance of smoking chimneys that punctuate the city's perimeter, the city centre offers another view, being a beguiling muddle of architecture from old wooden houses to huge Soviet housing estates.

Tourist Information Centre. Laisvės Aikštė 11. Tel: (8-45) 50 80 81. www.panevezystic.lt

Dailės Galerija (Art Gallery)

Avoid the dreadful modern paintings as you enter and head straight up the stairs, where you'll be greeted by a large, extraordinary and quite beautiful collection of international ceramics, from the dangerously cute to the outright strange. Run by a group of wonderful old ladies, the place holds a fairly prestigious ceramics festival every year, and the best work is displayed for the following 12 months.

Respublikos 3. Tel: (84-5) 58 48 02. Open: 11am–6pm. Closed: Mon & Tue. Admission charge.

Fotografijos Galerija (Photographic Gallery)

Just two small rooms focusing almost entirely on the work of contemporary Lithuanian photographers. Not too inspiring, but you can buy postcards of 19th-century Panevėžys.

Vasario 16-osios 11. Tel: (8-45) 46 75 51. Open: 11am–6pm. Closed: Mon & Tue. Admission charge.

Garsas

The contemporary creative focal point of the city. Here you'll find an excellent cinema showing films in English with Lithuanian subtitles, a bar, lots of contemporary individuals with the sort of hair and clothes one generally

The symbol of Panevėžys – the crab

St Peter and Paul's Church, Panevėžys

A NARROW ESCAPE

On 25 March 2001, the last ever scheduled narrow gauge train service of the once large Lithuanian narrow gauge railway network made its final official run along the 19th-century track between Panevėžys, Anykščiai and Rubikiai. Running at an enormous loss, the service was forced to close, but thanks to a handful of enthusiasts the line was saved from extinction and is still in operation. Now, for festive occasions at least, narrow gauge trains still run up and down it. Pulled by a handful of Soviet-built TU2 locomotives, the rolling stock can also be rented for any event from a wedding to part of the itinerary for an enthusiast's holiday. The so-called **Aukštaitijos Siaurasis Geležinkelis** (Aukštaitija Narrow Gauge Railway) runs through some marvellous scenery.
Aukštaitijos Siaurasis Geležinkelis. Geležinkelio 23, Panevėžys. Tel: (8-45) 57 71 27. www.siaurukas.eu

associates with cultural centres, and even a night club. You can also check your email in the building if you wish.
Respublikos 30. Tel: (8-45) 46 88 33. Open: 11.30am–11.30pm.

Kraštotyros Muziejus (Ethnographic Museum)

A really fine collection on three floors featuring archaeological exhibits downstairs, costumes, guns, recreated households and the most extraordinarily ornate wooden Russian telephone on the next floor up, and a menagerie of stuffed animals, including a rather large butterfly collection, above that.
Vasario 16-osios 23. Tel: (8-46) 56 19 73. Open: 10am–5pm. Closed: Sun & Mon. Admission charge.

Šiauliai

Although most people only visit Šiauliai due to its proximity to the Hill of Crosses, it's actually a rather vibrant city with lots to offer and deserves a visit in its own right. A place with a rich history and a bright future, Šiauliai is the fourth largest city in Lithuania with a population of around 135,000. It was first mentioned in historical documents in the mid-16th century, although there had been a settlement here since the 13th century. Šiauliai really came into its own in the 19th century with the construction of the Riga-Tilsit road and the Liepaja-Warsaw railway. At that time, major industries were established here, including Frenkelis' leatherworks business.

Today, the economy of the city is still dominated by leather processing, but other industries also thrive and 90 per cent of the goods, which include foodstuff and drinks, are exported to Western European countries. One of the major reconstructions that changed the whole feel of the city was the conversion of Vilniaus into a pedestrianised zone in the mid-1970s. This was a very innovative move at the time and attracted much interest both within the country and without. Recently completely renovated, Vilniaus is now one of the most attractive boulevards in the country. Smart shops, restaurants and cafés line the street, and overall there's a positive and progressive feel to the city. Šiauliai also boasts a number of unusual museums, of which the following is by no means a complete list.

Tourist Information Centre. Vilniaus 213. Tel: (8-41) 52 31 10. www.siauliai.lt

Amber jewellery can be bought in many outlets in Šiauliai

The cathedral in Šiauliai

Dviračių Muziejus (Bicycle Museum)
Not unlike the city's Radio and Television Museum (*see below*), this charming collection of two-wheelers gets its inspiration from one of the city's industries. A museum that grew out of Šiauliai's Vairas bicycle factory, this intriguing diversion includes 259 exhibits, of which 73 are actual bicycles.
Vilniaus 139. Tel: (8-41) 52 43 95. Open: Wed, Thur & Fri 10am–6pm, Sat & Sun 11am–5pm. Closed: Mon & Tue. Admission charge.

Fotografijos Muziejus (Photography Museum)
The museum is set over two floors. In the upstairs area you'll find a collection of photographic equipment doing its best to catalogue the history of photography. The ground floor acts as an exhibition space and features a mix of permanent and temporary exhibitions.
Vilniaus 140. Tel: (8-41) 52 43 96. Open: 10am–6pm. Closed: Mon & Tue. Admission charge.

Katinų Muziejus (Cat Museum)
A staggering 10,000-plus cat-related exhibits are gathered together here by local feline enthusiast Vanda Kavaliauslkienė.
Žuvininkų 18. Tel: (8-41) 52 38 83. Open: 11am–5pm. Closed: Sun & Mon. Admission charge.

Radijo ir TV Muziejus (Radio and Television Museum)
A rather quirky museum containing some extraordinary pieces including a 19th-century musical box with musical bees striking bells, and a radio disguised as a toy robot. Also

interesting is the demonstration of the Morse code transmitter.

Vilniaus 174. Tel: (8-41) 52 43 99. Open: Wed–Fri 10am–6pm, Sat & Sun 11am–2pm. Closed: Mon & Tue. Admission charge.

Tytuvėnai Regional Park

About 40km (25 miles) south of Šiauliai, this regional park used to be a popular retreat for celebrities in the pre-war era. It's now concerned mainly with preserving the cultural and natural environment of the two Catholic centres of Tytuvėnai and Šiluva. The park is spread over 10,571ha (26,120 acres), with 56 per cent covered in forest and a large proportion of wetlands making it a perfect habitat for many species of birds. It's naturally a very popular destination for dedicated birdwatchers, and a number of special hides (watchtowers) have been built in the park to accommodate such visitors. There's also a number of lakes in this park, making it a good spot for fishing. Boats are available to rent, and some centres even offer water bicycles.

Tytuvėnai's famous chapel to St Mary is one of five sites in Europe where the apparition of the Virgin Mary is said to have been seen, making it an important pilgrimage site. The first Sunday in September is the day of the pilgrimage, and every year thousands make the journey from Tytuvėnai to Šiluva.

Tytuvėnai Regional Park. Miškininkų 3. *Tytuvėnai village. Tel: (8-97) 56 651. www.trp.lt*

VILIUS ORVYDAS

Vilius Orvydas (1952–92) was a champion of Lithuanian outsider art who, like most outsider artists, never knew it. The controversial Žemaitijan stone carver and mystic built an incredible garden on the grounds of his parents' smallholding during the latter period of the Soviet occupation using a combination of salvaged crosses, junk and carvings of his own making. Through the family's connections, the garden survived attempts to destroy it by the Communists, and it remains an extraordinary testament to the artist, who died prematurely of a heart attack in the very garden he built.

The Orvydas Garden can be visited during the day, and is well worth looking out for if you're driving in the area. Leaving a small donation with the Orvydas family is much appreciated. A fascinating documentary film about Vilius Orvydas' strange life is available in many shops on DVD. The 2001 film has English subtitles and is released by Garsų Pasaulis (*www.gpi.lt*).

Orvydas Garden. Just south of Salantai on highway 169 on the road to Plungė. Open: daylight hours.

Typical method of conveyance for lake fishermen

The Litvaks

The Lithuanian Jews were and still are known as Litvaks, a Yiddish-speaking community who called Lithuania *Lita* or *Líte*, and who recognised its borders as being similar to those of the borders of Lithuania during the reign of the Grand Duchy, stretching from Riga in the north down as far as southern Ukraine. By the 18th century Vilnius, or Vilna to a Litvak, had become the world centre of traditional religious (Talmudic) learning, and was consequently known as the Jerusalem of Lithuania, or Jerusalem of the North.

The first mention in the annals of an organised Jewish community in Vilnius is in 1568, when they were ordered to pay a poll tax. The next significant mention can be traced to February 1633, when the Jews of Vilnius were granted a charter of privileges, which permitted them to become involved in all branches of commerce and distilling, and in any crafts that were not subject to the guild organisations. The charter did, however, restrict their places of residence within the city.

The first half of the 17th century saw a steady growth in the Jewish community in Vilnius as immigrants arrived from Prague, Frankfurt and a number of Polish towns. At this time

The Jewish Cemetery in Vilnius

the total population of the city was around 15,000, of whom 3,000 or so were Jewish, often wealthy and educated. Over the course of some 700 years of Lithuanian history, this Jewish community expanded into a thriving and diverse culture.

A centre of Torah learning

The Lithuanian Jewish community made up only a small proportion of the international Jewish community, but by the beginning of the 17th century, Vilnius had already become one of the leading centres for rabbinical studies and was regarded as a centre for Torah learning and culture. Their position in this regard was unique among the Jewish communities worldwide. The Litvaks, in comparison to other European neighbours, also constituted a considerably smaller percentage of the domestic population, but they were renowned for the calibre of their rational, intellectual approach to learning and spiritual matters as well as in the conduct of their day-to-day affairs. Of the thousands of notable Jewish intellectuals throughout history, arguably the most famous was the Vilnius-born rabbinic scholar, the greatest the world has ever known, the Gaon of Vilna, Eyliohu son of Shloyme-Zalmen (1720–97).

The Holocaust

The most terrible era for the Litvaks was during the Holocaust in Europe, with the Jewish community sustaining devastating losses at the hands of its occupiers. Over 95 per cent of the Jewish community was murdered. The Nazi regime is responsible for the annihilation of the Lithuanian Jews, their culture and the destruction of the Litvak legacy.

FIND OUT MORE

Apart from Paneriai (*see pp58–9*) just west of Vilnius, the following, all in Vilnius, are worth visiting:

Centre for Tolerance Art exhibitions, cultural events, seminars and conferences.
Naugarduko 10/2. Tel: (8-5) 231 23 56. www.jmuseum.lt

Chabad Lubavitch Centre Preserving and promoting Litvak life. The only place in Vilnius that can organise kosher food.
Šaltinių 12. Tel: (8-5) 215 03 87.

Holocaust Museum An essential part of any trip to Vilnius.
Paměnkalnio 12. Tel: (8-5) 262 07 30.

Jewish Community of Lithuania One of the best places to meet surviving Litvaks. Publishers of the English-language Jewish newspaper *Jerusalem of Lithuania*.
Pylimo 4. Tel: (8-5) 261 30 03. www.litjews.org

Synagogue The only one left, dating from 1904.
Pylimo 39 Tel: (8-5) 261 25 23.

Vilnius Yiddish Institute Brimming with academic activity. Warm welcomes to all who visit.
Old Campus Vilnius University (Daukanto Courtyard). Tel: (8-5) 268 71 87. www.judaicvilnius.com

Eastern Lithuania

Eastern Lithuania is dominated by tracts of beautiful landscape punctuated with small towns and national parks offering historical and specialist museums, a variety of activities and great natural beauty. This is a great area for touring, stopping off in pretty villages, and just admiring the scenery. The pace of life is slow and the people friendly, welcoming and eager to share their surroundings. Choose from a range of activities including walking, riding, swimming, driving, canoeing and a whole host of other fun things to do.

Aukštaitija National Park

At over 400sq km (155sq miles), the immense and truly wonderful Aukštaitija National Park is the main rural attraction in eastern Lithuania. A Mecca for water lovers, cyclists, ramblers and, in the winter, skiers, the park is a fabulous mixture of dense woodland and over 100 pristine lakes. Some of its woods are the remnants of

The bee-keeping museum at Stripeikiai in Aukštaitija National Park

ancient forests that once covered a large part of the region, and the park is full of rare plants.

The park is also known for its rich cultural heritage. Among the hills of Taurapilis, Ginučiai Puziniskiai, Linkmenys and Vajuonis are found 106 archaeological and architectural features, including the remains of fortifications from the 12th to the 15th centuries. The park area also includes over 100 small villages, many of which only contain a few farmsteads. These ancient settlements were made up of several buildings comprising a main house constructed perpendicular to the street with the cattle shed immediately behind. Farmsteads also had a granary with a cellar and a separate barn. Many fine examples of the local styles of buildings can be found in the villages of Ginučiai, Šakališkė and Kretuonys.

Eastern Lithuania

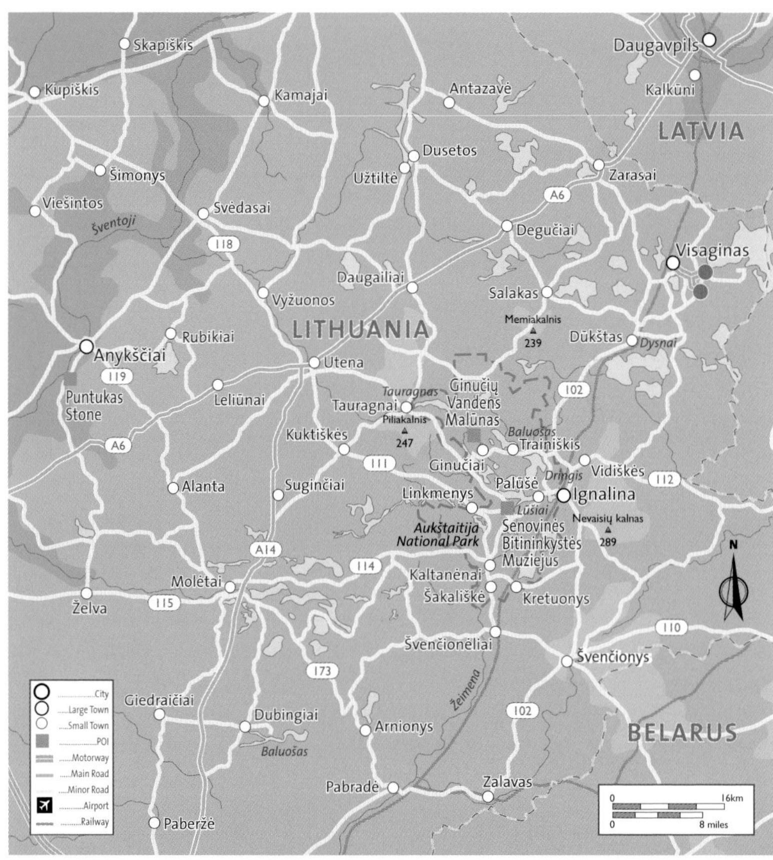

The old machinery is still the most reliable

Other attractions include Dringis, at 721ha (1,780 acres) the largest lake in the park, and the 60.5m (198ft) deep Tauragnas Lake, the deepest in Lithuania. Baluošas Lake features seven islands, one of which has a little lake of its own. Of the 30 or so rivers inside the park, the Žeimena is the most beautiful, although the smaller ones, notably Kriauna, Lukna, Buka and Šventelė all have their own natural charm and beauty.

Of the many towns located inside the park, the small village of Palūšė is both the most popular and the unofficial capital. Palūšė still boasts a spectacular wooden church with a rare free-standing bell tower dating back to 1750. Palūšė is the starting point for most of the tourist routes, both shorter and longer walks, plus rowing boat trips on the lakes and connecting streams.

Aukštaitija National Park Authority. Palūšė. Tel: (8-386) 531 35. www.anp.lt

Ginučiai

The diminutive one-street village of Ginučiai is home to a surprisingly large number of attractions, including its famous water mill. Of the six water mills inside the borders of the Aukštaitija National Park (the others being in Pakasas, Gaveikėnai, Pakretuonė, Minčia and Brukninė) this remains the only one with its original, working equipment. The Ginučiai mill is nearly 200 years old, and a visit here conjures up the sounds and images of a bygone age. As well as grinding wheat, the mill generated electricity for the entire village until 1968. The former purpose is celebrated in the mill's Bread Museum, where visitors can not only see how good old-fashioned country loaves are made but are also encouraged to make some of their own.

Close to the village the lakes of Sravinaitis, Baluošas and Almajas are all hugely popular places to fish, and you can swim and rent boats in the area too. If you don't mind the fact that the mill is allegedly haunted by none other than the Devil himself, you can also stay here for peanuts in one of the beautifully renovated, attached apartments. The mill also features a popular restaurant. *Ginučių Vandens Malūnas (Ginučiai Water Mill). Ginučiai. Tel: (8-383) 52 891. Open: 10am–6pm, Sun 10am–3pm. Closed: Mon. Admission charge.*

Palūšė

The tiny hamlet of Palūšė boasts the oldest wooden church in Lithuania, constructed in 1750 and built, so the legend goes, by Reverend Juozapas Bazilauskas using nothing but an axe. The Tourist Information Centre here is extremely helpful and also provides accommodation in winter and summer. There is a restaurant within the complex, Aukštaičių Užeiga, which can seat up to 100 people at a time in summer and offers live music during the weekends. During the winter a dining room with a capacity of 20 is also available.

From Palūšė you can go on day-trips by boat from Lūšiai Lake, hire bicycles or simply go for long walks in the breathtaking surrounding countryside. Other activities on offer include windsurfing, kayaking, canoeing, skiing (in winter), orienteering and tennis, to name just a few. Ignalina is within walking and cycling distance.

The ethnographic villages of Šakarva and Trainiškis are nearby, as well as the sturdy oak tree on Baluošas Lake with its mighty 6m (20ft) wide trunk. You can also relax on the public beach at Gavys Lake or enjoy the impressive views from the top of the famous, 175m (574ft) summit of Ledakalnis Hill.

Whatever you're into, this region of hills, lakes and forests is the perfect 'get-away-from-it-all' destination.

A forest track near Palūšė

The famous 18th-century wooden Church of St Joseph in Palūšė

Senovinės Bitininkystės Muziejus (Ancient Beekeeping Museum)
Set up by local fanatic Bronius Kazlas to teach visitors about the history and methods of beekeeping in Lithuania as well as to explain a little of the importance of bees to the pagan Lithuanian state, this extraordinary museum is located in the oldest village in the park and is more than worth a visit. Among the many beehives and other bee-related paraphernalia on display, visitors are treated to an educational roller coaster of a ride. The role of bees in ancient civilisations is covered, the fables of Lithuanian bee gods are revealed, and visitors are shown how to protect their honey from hungry bears. It all sounds rather strange, which indeed it is, but this is Lithuania after all, where bees are still treated with the utmost respect. The Lithuanian word for death, *mirtis*, is only used in reference to humans and bees. The Lithuanian word *bičiulis*, which translates as 'bee friend', is a particularly warm and personal word to denote a very close friend.
Stripeikiai village. Tel: (8-386) 36 210. Open: 10am–7pm. Closed: Mon. Admission charge.

Ignalina

Ignalina is a small town immediately east of the Aukštaitija National Park. Surrounded by numerous lakes and forests, with a population of over 7,500 people, Ignalina is the administrative centre of this district of the same name. During the second half of the 19th century, the Warsaw to St Petersburg railway was built directly through the town, increasing its significance on the global stage. The presence of a train station in the town also means that Ignalina is often the first place tourists discover when visiting the region. Perhaps the best example of a slightly run-down post-Soviet Lithuanian rural town in this guidebook, Ignalina offers little in the way of comfort for the Western traveller, with just two average restaurants and almost no sights. Its biggest claim to fame is its Winter Sports Centre, which attracts hordes of ski enthusiasts in season as well as other sports fans who use the place to take advantage of its excellent lakeside location.

Tourist Information Centre. Ateities 18a. Tel: (8-386) 52 597. www.ignalina.lt

Etninės Kultūros Centras (Ethno Culture Centre)

The Guggenheim it is not, but if you are looking for an authentic, low-budget insight into local art and culture then this place is highly recommended. Among the walls of local art find some wonderful historical photographs and examples of local folk craft.

Taikos 11, Tel: (8-386) 53 147.
Open: 8am–5pm. Closed: Sat & Sun. Admission charge.

Anykščiai

A settlement of some 13,500 people, rich in literary heritage and countryside traditions, the small town of Anykščiai has never been a major holiday destination in itself, but with the added attractions of a nearby nature reserve and horse museum, the tallest church in Lithuania and one of the few industrial tourism attractions in the country, the town warrants further investigation.

VISAGINAS

Just 35km (22 miles) northeast of Ignalina and worth a quick visit if you've got time on your hands is the remarkable town of Visaginas. Cut out of an area of dense Lithuanian forest in the few years following 1975 when it was officially founded, the 30,000 or so souls who make up the population of the town (which was originally called Sniečkus after a former leader of the Lithuanian Communist Party) were, or are the children of, Russian-speaking people who were brought to Lithuania to help build and maintain the Ignalina Nuclear Power Plant, currently shutting down, a process that will be complete at the end of 2009. An entirely Soviet city, built along Utopian lines and a real treat for anyone with an interest in things Soviet, Visaginas has a few basic restaurants and bars, a couple of small clubs and even a couple of hotels. The INPP Information Centre is also worth having a look at, featuring a model of the world's former largest nuclear power plant plus all manner of information on it and the people who work in it. Visaginas is also the home of the extraordinarily different Visagino Country music festival (*see p27*).

www.visaginas.lt

INPP Information Centre. Tel: (8-386) 29 911. Open: 8am–4pm. Closed: Sat & Sun (visits must be arranged in advance). www.iae.lt

The town's major sights can be covered in just an hour or two. Unmissable in more ways than one is the twin-towered, red-brick, neo-Gothic **Church of St Matthew (Šv Mato Neogotikinė Bažnyčia)** on Vilniaus just west of the town's square, Baranausko Aikštė. At a lofty 79m (260ft), Lithuania's allegedly tallest church was built between 1899 and 1909, and is perhaps most notable for the glass cases built into the walls surrounding the building, each one containing exquisite wooden carvings depicting the Stations of the Cross.

Close to the church, just east of the road bridge crossing the Šventoji River, the town's literary achievements are honoured by two statues of Anykščiai's greatest sons, the authors **Antanas Baranauskas and Antanas Žukauskas** (who wrote under the pen-name Vienuolis). A museum dedicated to the writers is also situated here (*Vienuolio 4. Tel: (8-381) 58 015. Open: 9am–6pm. Admission charge*).

The Church of St Matthew

Exactly 10km (6¼ miles) from the town centre is the **Puntukas Stone (Puntuko Akmuo)**, a huge remnant of prehistoric glacial drift, into which the faces of the two Lithuanian airborne heroes Darius and Girėnas (*see p84*) were carved in 1943 to mark the 10th anniversary of their deaths. The stone, located in a pine forest, is a popular meeting place in spring and summer, and forms the backdrop for every wedding photograph taken in the area.

The **Šventoji River**, which divides the town in two, is fast running, and offers excellent entertainment for the canoeing fraternity.

For information on the many other sights and sensations in and around Anykščiai, including information on a cuisine tour of the area, contact the Tourist Information Centre.

Tourist Information Centre. Gegužės 1. Tel: (8-381) 59 177. www.anyksciai.lt

Anykščių Vynas (Anykščiai Wine)

In 1926, Balys Karazija, a student at the local agricultural college, started making wines from local fruits and berries in the traditional way in a red brick building just off Anykščiai's main square. Twelve years later his *Birutė* took the Grand Prize at the 1938 Paris

Exhibition. Surviving the communists more or less intact, what later became Anykščių Vynas (Anykščiai Wine) now produces a staggering 12,000 bottles of wine every hour, as well as a number of spirits, liqueurs and fruit juices, all on a total of five production lines. One of the pioneers of industrial tourism in Lithuania, Anykščių Vynas organises tours of their factory for groups of three to fifty people. The tour consists of an historical overview of the company, a look around the entire plant, from the huge bins where lorries dump the local fruits, through the fruit presses, tanks and finally the fascinating automated bottling process, and finishing off rather nicely with a tasting session in a sumptuous room hidden away in the basement. Note that tours are conducted in Lithuanian, and visitors need to bring an interpreter. They also need to book in advance.

Dariaus ir Girėno 8. Tel: (8-381) 50 233. www.anyksciu-vynas.lt

HORSING AROUND

The only one of its kind in the country, the unusual Horse Museum (Arklio Muziejus) is located just 6km (3¾ miles) outside the town of Anykščiai. Founded in 1978, the museum explains the importance of the horse to the economy and culture of Lithuania. Eight different buildings display different equipment, tools and carriages used over the years. There's a play area for children, and there are opportunities to ride a horse or go for a ride in a horse-drawn carriage down the romantic 12km (7½-mile) Stallion Path. A festival of folklore and sports, Run, Stallion, Run, is held annually here over the first weekend in June.

Niūronys village. Tel: (8-381) 51 722. Open: 9am–6pm. Admission charge.

Fountains in the Šventoji River, Anykščiai

Getting away from it all

The abundance and diversity of Lithuanian nature is absolutely breathtaking. The country has five main national parks and many regional parks and nature reserves. For travellers looking for respite from the hustle and bustle of crowded tourist sites, these are the places to visit. A number of resorts and retreats also offer cures for all types of ailments, physical and emotional, along with that much-needed space for relaxing and recharging one's batteries.

The landscapes of Lithuania are not only beautiful, but also diverse. The scenery in the eastern Aukštaitija region, with its chains of lakes, contrasts greatly with the high sand dunes of the Curonian Spit or the dense forests of the Dzūkija region. The five national parks in Lithuania are the Aukštaitija National Park (Aukstaitijos Nacionalinis Parkas), the Curonian Spit National Park (Kuršių Nerijos Nacionalinis Parkas), the Dzūkija National Park (Dzūkijos Nacionalinis Parkas), the Trakai Historical National Park (Trakų Istorinis Nacionalinis Parkas) and the Žemaitija National Park (Žemaitijos Nacionalinis Parkas). Each park has its own distinctive natural features. Most areas of the national parks in Lithuania allow visitors, and some even permit camping in designated areas. However, there are certain reserved areas within the national parks that aren't open to visitors unless they are accompanied by the park staff.

The parks offer visitors not only an opportunity to take in some breathtaking sights, including the flora and fauna, but also the chance to gain some cultural understanding, as they provide insight into the Lithuanian culture and people.

THE LAND OF THE FOLK

Like the more famous Germanic folktales, Lithuanian folklore is full of tales of confrontation between human beings and nature. There are stories of people getting lost in dark forests with menacing trails, while others have difficulties with mysterious lakes or battle menacing beasts.

The heroes of these stories, however, never come across as victors over nature. Their victory is always achieved by respecting the land and listening to the animals. As a result of this respect shown to nature, every creature, big or small, tries to repay the protagonist in some manner. Some animals reward the heroes with unusual abilities, while others carry out difficult tasks for them as an expression of their gratitude. Most Lithuanians today still respect their land and display a great regard for it. It's part of their national identity, a fact expressed in their folk music, dance and art (*see pp24–5*).

If none of that appeals to you, you can always visit the parks simply for the opportunity they provide for rest and recuperation. If you're looking for peace and tranquillity, a Lithuanian national park is the place to go.

Aukštaitija National Park

Aukštaitija National Park, established in 1974, was the first of Lithuania's national parks. This protection has helped the park sustain many species of plants and animals, including a single specimen of the rare ghost orchid.

Situated in the northeastern region of the country, its proximity to Vilnius (only 70km/44 miles to the north), makes it a popular destination. You can either hire a car (*see p180*) or take a bus to get there. Spread over 40,570ha (100,300 acres), this natural paradise is made up of rolling hills, 102 lakes, both large and small, and 34 rivers and streams. Most of the lakes lie next to each other, forming a sort of unlinked chain. Around 100 settlements dot the park, most of them housing a few farming families. Most of these settlements are said to be over 2,000 years old.

Any description of this area of the country must contain the word 'sparkling'. This amount of water provides many opportunities for water-

National Park of Aukštaitija

based activities, such as canoeing and fishing; note that it's necessary to purchase a fishing licence, available from any of the tourist information centres or the nearest forestry office. The best way to travel within the park is by boat, as the numerous forest paths inevitably lead to the water's edge. This way, you can explore the more remote and untouched areas.

There are, however, also countless options for beautiful lakeside walks and opportunities to revel in the stunning scenery of the rolling hills and beautiful forests that surround the lakes. A walk up to the top of Ladakalnis Hill is well worth the effort for a bird's-eye view of the entire park.

Quirky and often humorous woodcarvings are a feature in many woods and forests

The area is great for bird watching, too. Along the edge of the water, you can often spot birds like black-throated divers, black storks, curlews and snipes feeding.

In the winter months, the park also offers many adventure activities, including cross-country skiing, ice-fishing, sledging and horse- and sleigh-riding.

Ignalina is a small town just east of the Aukštaitija National Park. Palūšė is a village close by and also the administrative centre for the park. Both places offer accommodation and good local cuisine, and either would make a good base out of which to explore the park.

Aukštaitija National Park. Tel: (8-386) 53 135. www.anp.lt

Curonian Spit National Park

The Curonian Spit is a unique piece of land in the west of the country on the Baltic coast. The national park was created to protect the unique ecosystem of the Curonian Spit, a peninsula that separates the Curonian Lagoon from the Baltic Sea. The park covers an area of 18,000ha (44,480 acres).

On one hand, the Curonian Spit is the land of fishermen, primitive nature and sand dunes. On the other, it's also the place for a tranquil, restful holiday. A lot of new hotels have been built in the last decade, and older ones renovated, attracting more tourists each year, not only from within Lithuania but from around the world. Tourism

View of the Curonian Spit

has, in fact, become the area's main industry. Organising leisure activities in some form or another for tourists is the main livelihood of the 2,700 local people who live in Neringa.

If you get tired of sunbathing on the soft white sands in summer, you can go windsurfing, yachting or boating on the Curonian Lagoon. During the winter, swimming pools are heated, the resorts are quieter and calmer and less packed. A few cafés and bars stay open in the winter, making the area a year-round destination. You can also visit the Fisherman's Ethnographic Homestead, the Curonian Spit Livelihood Exhibition, the Thomas Mann House, the Witches' Hill with its carved wooden sculptures, the Amber Gallery, an ethnographic cemetery and many more interesting places which are open throughout the year (*see pp103–7 for details*).

The Spit is a good getaway destination from Palanga, a popular resort some 30km (19 miles) north on the coast, which can become a bit of a party town in the summer. There are two regular ferries onto the spit from Klaipėda, making it an easy and hassle-free destination for an afternoon visit or a few days' stay if you wish to get away from it all for a little longer. You can relax on one of the many pristine blue-flag beaches, drive around the

Wonderful stretches of pale sandy beaches mark the Lithuanian seaside

area in a car (*see pp106–7*), or take an organised cruise around the Curonian Lagoon (*see p105*). The two tourist information centres in Neringa give you ample information about local events through literature and booklets. You can make reservations for hotels or private bed-and-breakfast facilities through these centres as well.
Curonian Spit National Park.
Tel: (8-464) 02 257. www.nerija.lt

Dzūkija National Park

The Dzūkija National Park is close enough to both Vilnius and Kaunas to make it very convenient for a short break. It is only 100km (62 miles) southwest of Vilnius and a bit less than that south of Kaunas. This makes it less than an hour and a half's drive from either city. Travelling around the park by car is the most convenient and comfortable method of getting around. The excellent road network provides easy access to the main areas of Marcinkonys and Merkinė.

Organised bus excursions to the park are another option. Detailed information is available at all tourist offices and information centres.

Once there, you can take advantage of the numerous walking and biking trails in the park. The park spreads over 55,900ha (138,100 acres) of southern Lithuania, with 43,700ha (108,000 acres) of the area under forest cover.

Most of it (about 95 per cent) lies in the district of Varėna, with a small part in the Alytus district (4 per cent) and a tiny slither in the district of Lazdijai (just 1 per cent).

The park was founded on 23 April 1991, with the principal objective of protecting, managing and utilising one of the richest natural and cultural territories within Lithuania. It's the largest protected area in Lithuania, with over 30 rivers and streams. Its pine forests are rich in mushrooms and blueberries. But its unique dunes are its core attraction.

The area also contains the remains of some Stone Age settlements. The mounds and hills around Merkinė and Liškiava, in particular, are famous both for their history as well as for their scenic views. The village of Merkinė dates back to the 14th century and is situated at the confluence of two rivers, the Nemunas and the Merkys. The castle hill here offers spectacular views of the Nemunas Valley.

The villages of Musteika, Zervynos, Dubininkas and Lynežeris have been listed as national architectural monuments. The traditional layout of these villages, with their typical architecture, has been preserved to this day. Many of the local inhabitants still pursue their traditional crafts of pottery making, woodcarving and weaving.

This rare combination of cultural and natural sights provides the tourist with an array of choices. The lakes are good

Trees abound in Lithuania's national parks

PLANT KINGDOM, ANIMAL PLANET

The pine trees that dominate the Dzūkija region protect and nurture many rare and endangered species. In fact, the unique geographical position has determined the region's diversity of species. A combination of sandy plains in the southeast with Dzūkija's moraine highlands and river valleys, along with the area's unique climate, has created the perfect habitat for these rare species. The species list of the region includes 750 types of higher plants, nearly 300 mushrooms, over 200 lichens, 40 mammals, including elk, deer, wild boar, fox and wolf, 48 bird species, 2 kinds of reptiles, 3 amphibians, 3 fish, 2 molluscs, 41 insects and a type of leech. Of these, 217 species found in this area are on the protected list. These include the eagle owl, the bulbiferous coralwort, the Machaon butterfly and the smooth snake.

Sign welcoming you to Žemaitija National Park

for swimming, the forests for exploring and mushroom-picking, and stretches of the rivers Ūla and Merkys for canoeing (make sure to purchase a permit for the River Ūla, which is available from the park administration). There are also four cycling tracks, six walking and hiking trails and fifteen campsites. You would have to work very hard to be bored here.

Dzūkija National Park. Tel: (8-310) 44 466. www.dzukijosparkas.lt

Trakai Historical National Park

The Trakai Historical National Park covers about 8,200ha (20,260 acres) and its Island Castle (*see pp63–5*), located in the town of Trakai, is one of the most famous sites in Lithuania. This Gothic castle is situated on an island in the middle of the spectacular Galvė Lake. The town of Trakai itself was founded in the 14th century and was the second capital of the Lithuanian Grand Duke Kęstutis. Today it remains a beautiful town.

There are 32 lakes within the park, which means that almost one-fifth of the area is water. It is therefore not surprising that many of the activities the park offers are water-based (*see pp64–5*). Being so close to the capital makes the area an easy get-away destination for those who don't have the time to travel too far from Vilnius, and due to its close proximity to Vilnius, it is the most visited of the national parks in Lithuania. Travelling to Trakai from Vilnius is not complicated as there are many buses leaving from the city centre at regular intervals. You can ask at any tourist

information centre for details of timings and routes. It's also easily accessible by car.
Trakai Historical National Park. Tel: (8-528) 53 840. www.seniejitrakai.lt

Žemaitija National Park

The landscape of the Žemaitija National Park was formed some 12,000 years ago by ice and receding glaciers. These climatic conditions created its distinctive features of rounded hills, deep and shallow lakes, and moraine ridges. There are 26 post-glacial lakes and 32 streams in the park. The largest lake in Žemaitija is Lake Plateliai (*see pp136–7*). The park is a watershed to three river basins, the Minija, the Batuva and the Venta. The dense forests contain a huge variety of trees, including pine, spruce, birch, alder and oak.

This national park is also famous for its cultural heritage. The 3,000 people that still live in the area have preserved their own particular dialect, customs and characteristics. There are many museums here, too, including the Woodcraft Museum in Godeliei, the Literary Museum in both Bukantė and Žemaičių Kalvarija, and the Art Gallery in Babrungėnai.

Sunlight streams through the trees, creating a picturesque canvas of light and shade

Activities available in the park include horse riding in Plokštinė, which is an easy and relaxing way to enjoy the countryside. You can also hire bikes in Plateliai and take advantage of the three cycling tracks in the park, or hire a boat in Plateliai to either explore the lakes or go fishing.

The Žemaitija National Park is only 33km (20 miles) from the town of Plungė. There are buses and trains connecting Plungė to other towns and cities in Lithuania. The Žemaitija National Park Administration Centre and Visitor Centre is in Plateliai, which can be reached by car or bus. The centre provides information on museums, sites of interest, festivals, accommodation and excursions in the park, and also issues fishing permits. *Žemaitija National Park. Tel: (8-448) 49 337. www.zemaitijosnp.lt*

Lake Plateliai

This lake is the largest and deepest in the western region of Lithuania. It covers an area of 1,200ha (2,965 acres) and at its deepest point is 47m (154ft). There are seven islands on the lake, each with its own legends and folklore.

There once stood a beautiful castle on the largest of the seven islands, but now only its ruins remain. Three of the islands and one of the peninsulas have been declared national natural monuments. The hills around the lake provide excellent views of the water and the islands in it. The forest and surrounding marshes are home to unique flora and fauna, and the lake landscape itself offers crystal-clear water, clean campsites and beautiful scenery.

Lakeside accommodation in the national parks

An abundance of apples in September

The region has many bays, peninsulas and walking routes that can be explored on foot, or by bike, boat or car. In the town of Plateliai itself there are shops, cafés, hotels, a petrol station and a post office, making it a good place to stop for the night, to relax, refuel and rejuvenate. The town also houses the management office of the Žemaitija National Park, the Local Authority office and Tourist Information Centre, so it's a good place to pick up information about the rest of the park.

DIVERSE AND RARE FAUNA IN THE ŽEMAITIJA NATIONAL PARK

A grand total of 189 different species of birds have been identified in the park, of which 48 are rare species, including the black stork, tern and corncrake. There are 49 species of mammals, 13 of which are protected, including the lynx, otter and white hare. There are 11 species of bats here and 26 species of fish, including rare members of the salmon family. Some have existed in Lake Plateliai since the post-glacial era. There are over 600 species of beetles and 640 species of butterflies, too.

Salantų Regioninis Parkas (Salantai Regional Park)

The very special Salantai Regional Park is in the northwest of the country, about 25km (15 miles) northeast of Palanga. It was set up to protect and preserve the natural ecosystem and cultural heritage in the valleys of the rivers Salantas, Erla and Minija. These beautiful old valleys contain springs, ravines and steep escarpments that offer outstanding views. Also interesting to see while you are here are boulders that have remained untouched by civilisation since the last Ice Age (12th–10th millennia BC). Most of these can be found around Šaukliai, Kulaliai and Igariai. Tourists come here for outdoor, mainly water, activities. Many come just for rafting on the River Minija, for which this body of water is famous, whilst others prefer the more leisurely water sport of fishing. Both the rivers Minija and Salantas, and the ponds at Mosėdis, offer excellent fishing.

Salantai Regional Park. Laivių 9, Salantai village. Tel: (8-445) 58 761.

A meandering river in Salantai Regional Park

The tranquil waters flow gently through the park

Shopping

In Lithuania you'll find many souvenir shops offering traditional products, amber and woodcarvings. The main cities provide the option of shopping in a wide range of international and local fashion houses, and there is also a good number of shops selling fine cosmetics and perfumes. Whether you're looking for local products, souvenirs, handbags, fur or leather, you'll find it in Lithuania. Every Lithuanian town and city also has at least one traditional market selling everything from smoked sausage to Chinese underpants. A trip to one of these extraordinary places is more than worth the effort.

Regular shopping hours are weekdays 10am–7pm and Saturdays 10am–3pm. Some shops are open on Sundays as well. Food stores are usually open between 8am and 10pm, and some supermarkets are open until midnight. There are also a few shops which are open 24 hours. The larger malls springing up all over the country are usually open seven days a week from 10am to 10pm, sometimes even longer.

Amber brings good luck

Amber

Baltic amber, as much as 50 million years old, is a tourist attraction in itself in Lithuania. It's been considered the most valuable Lithuanian export for centuries, traded as far as ancient Rome and even being found in the Pharaoh's tombs in Egypt. An amber souvenir is said to bring good luck, and is especially valuable if there's an insect trapped inside the resinous gem. Vilnius' old town and anywhere along the coast are the best places to buy it.

Fashion

Not surprisingly, all three major Lithuanian cities have the most cosmopolitan choice in fashion, with a growing number of upmarket international labels represented. However, it's always worth scouting around in smaller cities and towns, as you never know when you may come across something unusual, which is of course the real joy of shopping when you're on holiday.

Souvenirs

There is a wide range of interesting souvenirs you can bring back from Lithuania. The country has a strong tradition of handicrafts, be it in woodcarving, linen or woven sashes. Beautiful handmade sashes represent a very old part of Lithuanian tradition; they used to be worn instead of belts. The array of colours used in these sashes reflects the Lithuanian appreciation for bright hues. They are no longer used solely as belts, but are available in many lengths and widths, so you can make them into unusual interior decoration features. Handmade mittens and socks are another nice gift to take home. Knitted flax tablecloths are also extremely popular.

VILNIUS

Shopping in the centre of Vilnius is best experienced on foot. Head for Gedimino, Pilies, Didžioji and Aušros Vartų, the best of the bunch and brimming with shops selling everything from expensive clothes to high-quality amber jewellery, antiques, local art and books. If you're looking specifically for local craft and souvenirs, the best choice can be found along Pilies and Didžioji. Along Pilies there are many outdoor stalls which supply all types of souvenirs, including amber, woodcarvings, handmade toys and jewellery.

You can pick up souvenirs from the Soviet era

Amber

In and around the old town is considered the best place in Vilnius to buy the coveted Baltic amber (*gintaras*). However, do beware of fakes. If in doubt, buy amber only from stores providing a certificate of origin with the sale. The shops listed are all highly recommended.

Amber Museum Gallery
Šv Mykolo 8.
Tel: (8-5) 262 30 92.
Open: 10am–7pm.

Amber Sculpture Museum
Aušros Vartų 9.
Tel: (8-5) 262 52 41.
Open: Mon–Fri 10am–7pm, Sat 10am–5pm.
Closed: Sun.

Shop of Amber
Didžioji 6.

Art and handicrafts

Art salon
Stiklių 16.

Gallery Verpstė
Handicrafts.
Žydų 2.
Tel: (8-5) 262 58 87.

Keramikos Meno Centras
Ceramics.
Kauno 36/7.
Tel: (8-5) 216 03 72.

Linas
Linen.
Didžioji 11 and Stiklių 3.

Suvenyrai
Souvenirs.
Šv Jono 12.
Tel: (8-5) 261 15 97.

Vilnius Antique Centre
Dominikonų 16.
Tel: (8-5) 262 74 79.
Open: Mon–Fri 11am–7pm, Sat 11am–3pm.
Closed: Sun.

Vilniaus Juvelyrika
Jewellery.
Pilies 17.
Tel: (8-5) 261 04 69.

Books

Akademinė Knyga
Universiteto 4.
Tel: (8-5) 266 16 80.
Open: Mon–Fri 10am–7pm, Sat 10am–3pm.

French Bookshop
Didžioji 1.
Tel: (8-5) 262 05 17.

Humanitas
Vokiečių 2.
Tel: (8-5) 262 11 53.

Littera
Universiteto 3.
Tel: (8-5) 212 77 46.
Open: Mon–Fri 9am–6pm, Sat 10am–3pm.
Closed: Sun.

Oxford Centre
Trakų 5.
Tel: (8-5) 261 04 16.

Shopping centres

Try one of the modern malls listed below.

Akropolis
A vast shopping and entertainment centre in the north of the city featuring shops, restaurants, bars, bowling, cinemas and an ice rink.
Ozo 25.

Europa
Lots of classy shops close to the city centre. Also cafés and restaurants.
Konstitucijos 7a.

VCUP
A nicely restored Soviet-era shopping centre on the river.
Konstitucijos 16.

KAUNAS

The main shopping spine of the city is to be found along Vilniaus in the old town, running into Laisvės Alėja.

Antiques

Antikvariatas
Rotušės 29.
Tel: (8-37) 22 94 89.

Books

Knygų Alėja
Laisvės Alėja 29.
Tel: (8-37) 32 09 63.

Pegasas
Laisvės Alėja 75.
Tel: (8-37) 42 84 69.
Open: Mon–Fri 9am–7pm, Sat 10am–6pm.

Tūkstantis ir Viena Knyga
Vilniaus 11.
Tel: (8-37) 20 95 81.

Fashion

Aprangos Galerija
Laisvės Alėja 55.
Tel: (8-37) 20 08 13.

Baltman
Laisvės Alėja 49.
Tel: (8-37) 75 00 42.

Benetton
Laisvės Alėja 67.
Tel: (8-37) 32 23 95.

Monton
Laisvės 45.
Tel: (8-37) 40 75 62.

Food and drink

Arbata, Prieskoniai, Kava
Vilniaus 29.

IKI
Jonavos 3.
Tel: (8-37) 20 03 78.

Gifts and souvenirs

Dailė
Rotušės 1.

Kauno Langas
Valančiaus 5.
Tel: (8-37) 20 55 38.

Suvenyrai
Vilniaus 32.
Tel: (8-37) 22 51 26.
Open: Mon–Fri 10am–6.30pm, Sat & Sun 10am–5pm.

KLAIPĖDA

Klaipėda features a number of whimsical and quirky shops.

Bičių Korys
Delicious local honey.
Sukilėlių 18.
Tel: (8-46) 31 38 80.

Cronus
Leather goods.
Vytauto 3/28.
Tel: (8-46) 41 22 79.

Laimės Tiltas
Clocks and watches at reasonable prices.
Tiltų 4.
Tel: (8-46) 41 20 00.

Mažoji Indija
Exotic pieces from Africa and the East.
Tomo 16-1.
Tel: (8-46) 36 06 18.

Nautilus
Shells and coral.
Tomo 10.

Suvenyrų Pasaulis
Hand-painted clothes, wooden carvings and other unusual objects.
Aukštoji 5.
Tel: (8-46) 41 04 86.

ŠIAULIAI

The main street, Vilniaus, is where you'll find the majority of good shops.

Dorado
Plenty of choice here for gifts.
Vilniaus 215.
Tel: (8-41) 42 04 34.

Lėja
A good selection of accessory-type items.
Vytauto 110.
Tel: (8-41) 42 52 49.

Savex Galerija
An extraordinary and eclectic array of goods.
Vilniaus 251.
Tel: (8-41) 52 14 18.

Tourism Information Centre
Souvenirs and crafts.
Vilniaus 213.

TAX-FREE SHOPPING

In Lithuania it's possible for all non-EU passport holders to get a tax refund if they spend more than 200Lt in one store. However, this is only available in shops that display the sign 'Tax Free Shopping'. In these shops, ask for a tax money return form and a tax invoice. You must also remember to get a stamp on the invoice at your point of departure when you leave the country.

Amber

Legend and science tell different stories about the origins of amber. Lithuanian legend holds that amber originates from the tears of the sea goddess Jūratė. Jūratė fell in love with a mortal fisherman, Kastytis, and invited him to come and live under the sea in her beautiful amber castle. When Perkūnas, the god of thunder, found out about this love affair between goddess and mortal, he was very unhappy. In a fit of anger, he destroyed Jūratė's castle with a storm. Pieces of amber found today are supposed to be the remains of her castle and her tears.

Amber beads for sale

Science tells another, less romantic story of the origin of the precious resin. Approximately 40–50 million years ago, the earth got warmer, which led to an increase in the amount of resin secreted in the pine forests of Fennoscandia. This large land mass was later consumed by the Baltic Sea. The resin was then swept down the rivers to the sea, with its sticky properties sometimes catching an insect or even a lizard along the way. Deltaic deposits of this fossilised resin are what we know as amber and can be found in Lithuania, Poland, Sweden and Kaliningrad.

There are several museums in Lithuania illustrating the story of the evolution of amber. The largest collection of rare pieces of amber in the world can be found in the Tiškevičius Palace in the Botanical Park in the coastal resort of Palanga (*see p95*). This fine mansion was bought by Count Felix Tiškevičius in the 1850s and is a great setting for this fascinating museum. The exhibition is very well presented and gives a comprehensive and clear history of the origins of the substance. You can see 25,000 examples of the different types of amber, many with plants, animals and insects trapped inside. There's a

Some highly unusual amber pieces are for sale in Vilnius

magnificent array of jewellery and other items, too. For information about any of the other amber museums located throughout Lithuania, enquire at the local tourist offices for recommendations in their region.

Amber is popularly known as Baltic Gold and can still be found on the shores of the Baltic Sea, particularly after a storm. Although the majority of pieces are pure, the ones that contain the remains of an insect or a pine needle are the most valuable. Understandably, amber is the classic Lithuanian gift or souvenir, and its unique beauty does not wane over the years, nor is it subject to the fickle and dizzying changes of the fashion world. If you're not lucky enough to find a piece 'in the wild', there's a vast range of purchasable crafted pieces to choose from in shops throughout Lithuania, including necklaces, bracelets, rings and other jewellery, unusual ornaments and lamps.

Despite the oft-held assumption to the contrary, amber actually comes in a whole range of colours, the most common being the famous dark honey colour (from where it gets its nickname), but it's also found in shades of blue, deep red, orange, black, white, green and yellow. If in doubt about what you're getting, ask for a certificate of origin and authenticity for your purchase, as there are many fakes around.

Entertainment

*Lithuania has a rich cultural heritage in both classical and contemporary art, music and drama. Vilnius and Kaunas both have regular programmes of concerts and operas running throughout the year, including many jazz festivals (*see p27*). Folk music and dance are also an important part of the entertainment scene. In the cities across Lithuania, there is no shortage of mainstream nightlife, including a decent selection of clubs, bars and cafés.*

VILNIUS

Casinos

Grand Casino World
Vienuolio 4. Tel: (8-700) 55 599.

Cinemas

Almost all films are shown in their original language with Lithuanian subtitles. For more information, see *www.cinema.lt*

Coca Cola Plaza
Savanorių 7. Tel: 15 67.

Skalvija
Goštauto 2/15.
Tel: (8-5) 261 05 05.

Galleries

Art Academy Gallery
Pilies 44/2. Tel: (8-5) 261 20 94.

Artists' Palace
Rotušė, Didžioji 31.
Tel: (8-5) 261 75 72.

Contemporary Art Centre
Vokiečių 2. Tel: (8-5) 212 19 45.

Užupio Galerija
Užupio 3. Tel: (8-5) 231 23 18.

Nightlife

Brodvėjus
The combined bar, restaurant and nightclub Brodvėjus (Broadway) is one of the city's legends, and packs in a mixed crowd of happy locals and foreigners seven nights a week. Take your pick from one of two bars or chance your arm in the club space featuring nightly performances of both live music and DJs.
Mėsinių 4. Tel: (8-5) 210 72 08.
Open: Wed–Sat noon–5am, Sun & Mon noon–3am, Tue noon–4am.

Cozy
Cozy features a quality bar-restaurant on the ground floor which serves excellent food and is usually packed with the city's more sophisticated A-list characters. There's also a relaxed club space in the basement. Note that the basement club is only open on Thursday, Friday and Saturday nights.
Dominikonų 10. Tel: (8-5) 261 11 37.
Open: Mon–Thur 9am–2am, Fri 9am–4am, Sat 10am–4am, Sun 10am–2am.

Helios

A scintillating mix of good tunes and beautiful people in the old town's glitziest and most popular nightspot. Big and sweaty, the emphasis is on flashing lights, cocktails and having a good time. Look out for the special theme nights and the occasional fashion show.

Didžioji 28. Tel: (8-5) 261 50 40. Open: 11pm–5am. Closed: Sun–Wed.

Pabo Latino

Priced to keep all but a better class of clubber howling at the door, this is the choice spot for a wide range of well-heeled partygoers both local and foreign alike. Summer nights hail the opening of a fabulous courtyard that only adds to the overall exclusiveness of one of the capital's favourite places to forget the week and let it all hang out.

Trakų 3/2. Tel: (8-5) 262 10 45. Open: Fri–Sun 8pm–5am, Wed 8pm–1am, Thur 8pm–3am. Closed: Mon & Tue.

Sky Bar

The perfect opportunity to rub shoulders with everyone from retired German tourists to the occasional local celebrity in this 22nd-floor masterpiece. Quality service, a good cocktail list and an excellent music policy to boot. The views of the old town and the sun setting over Vilnius' concrete sleeping districts are truly outstanding.

Revel Hotel Lietuva, Konstitucijos 20. Tel: (8-5) 272 62 72. Open: Sun–Thur 4pm–1am, Fri & Sat 4pm–2.30am.

Opera, music and ballet

Opera and Ballet Theatre

Vienuolio 1. Tel: (8-5) 262 07 27.

View an exhibition at one of Vilnius' galleries, or here at the National Art Museum

The Three Muses outside the National Drama Theatre in Vilnius

Theatres

National Drama Theatre

Gedimino 4. Tel: (8-5) 262 97 71.

KAUNAS

Bowling

Straikas

Draugystės 6a.
Tel: (8-37) 40 90 00.

Casinos

Los Casino

Los Patrankos, Savanorių 124.
Tel: (8-37) 33 82 28.

Cinemas

Forum Cinemas

Akropolis, Karaliaus Mindaugo 49.
Tel: 15 67.

Galleries

Kauno Langas

Valančiaus 5. Tel (8-37) 20 55 38.

Meno Parkas

Rotušės Aikštė 27. Tel: (8-37) 33 71 67.

Nightlife

Amerika Pirtyje

A Kaunas institution featuring two dance floors for both techno and something less frenetic, as well as the occasional live music performance and maybe a saucy strip show. Sophisticated it isn't, but as you'll see from the masses of scantily clad people out to enjoy the venue's excesses, that's not really the point.

Vytauto 71. Tel: (8-37) 20 14 89.
Open: Mon & Tue 11am–5pm, Wed &

Thur 11am–2am, Fri 11am–4am, Sat 2pm–4am, Sun 8pm–2am.

BO

Just about the only bar in the country that doesn't feel ashamed to offer educated drinkers a scruffy setting, this outstanding institution comes with broken chairs, wobbly tables and an equally through-the-hedge-backwards-looking set of patrons. By far the best place in town to meet English-speaking youngsters who like a drink or two, this is quite possibly the best bar in Lithuania.
Muitinės 9-1. Tel: (8-37) 20 65 42. Open: Mon–Thur 9.30am–2am, Fri 9.30am–3am, Sat 3pm–3am, Sun 3pm–2am.

Los Patrankos

Attracting party animals from as far afield as Vilnius during the weekend, this large and energetic club has been packing them in since nobody can quite remember. The heaving, flashing, sweaty dance floor never fails to titillate, plus there are plenty of opportunities to sit around and watch the action if dancing isn't your thing.
Savanorių 124. Tel: (8-37) 33 82 28. Open: Tue–Thur 9pm–4am, Fri & Sat 9pm–6am, Sun 1pm–5pm. Closed: Mon.

Opera, music and ballet

Kaunas Philharmonic
Sapiegos 5. Tel: (8-37) 22 25 58.

Musical Theatre
Laisvės Alėja 91. Tel: (8-37) 22 71 13.

Kaunas' Musical Theatre

The Academic Drama Theatre in Kaunas

Theatres

Academic Drama Theatre
Laisvės Alėja 71.
Tel: (8-37) 20 76 93.

Puppet Theatre
Laisvės Alėja 87a. Tel: (8-37) 22 00 63.

KLAIPĖDA

Cinemas

Jūratė ir Kastytis
Taikos 105. Tel: (8-46) 34 28 57.

Concert halls

Philharmonic
Danės 19. Tel: (8-46) 41 05 76.

Galleries

Exhibition Hall
Aukštoji 3. Tel: (8-46) 31 44 43.

Fotogalerija
Tomo 7. Tel: (8-46) 41 04 02.

Parko Galerija
Turgaus 9. Tel: (8-46) 31 05 01.

Nightlife

Kalifornija
The city's top nightspot for unadulterated working-class fun, this veritable meat market stuck out in the suburbs attracts everyone from local Barbie doll look-alikes to visiting Filipino sailors in need of more than just a drink. Occasionally a little edgy thanks to the local lads who come here after drinking too much vodka, Kalifornija is recommended, but only to those who like their evenings spiced up with the occasional crowd of staggering testosterone.
Laukininkų 17. Tel: (8-46) 22 97 35.
Open: Sun–Thur 10pm–7am, Fri & Sat 10am–8am.

Kurpiai
A fairly small and highly recommended live jazz club in the heart of the old town with the addition of a decent menu, Kurpiai's reputation as one of

the best nights out in Klaipėda is well deserved. Although the new smoking laws mean it's no longer necessary to bring a gas mask on a Friday or Saturday evening, the place still gets extremely hot and crowded.
Kurpių 1a. Tel: (8-46) 41 05 55. Open: Tue–Sat noon–2am, Sun & Mon noon–midnight.

Memelis
Inside a wonderfully restored building, find three floors of fun, beer brewed on the premises and a fine menu to help soak it all up. Memelis is your classic Lithuanian treat, featuring every possibility from food to drink and a nightclub that can be rather hit or miss. Located close to a few other good nightspots, this one's always worth checking out.
Žvejų 4. Tel: (8-46) 40 30 40. Open: Tue–Thur noon–2am, Fri & Sat noon–4am, Sun & Mon noon–midnight.

Theatres

Drama Theatre
Teatro 2. Tel: (8-46) 31 44 53.
Musical Theatre
Danės 19. Tel: (8-46) 39 74 04.

A LITTLE BIT COUNTRY...

At the height of the Cold War during the academic year 1973–4, a small group of Lithuanian students would get together to play, listen to and talk about music. Two of them, medical student Virgis Stakėnas (1953–) and agricultural student Vytautas Babravičius (aka Simas, 1952–), would go on to become pioneers of a very Lithuanian type of Country & Western music. The first Lithuanian Country & Western band was Deficitai (The Deficits), founded by Simas in 1979. Deficitai were an all-acoustic band who played the peculiar mixture of country and folk that would go on to symbolise Lithuania's country music genre.

Lithuania's most notorious country figure is the larger-than-life medical school dropout Virgis Stakėnas, who swapped his stethoscope for a Stetson longer ago than he cares to remember and who hasn't looked back since. A tireless promoter of the cause, Stakėnas has released well over a dozen albums since turning professional in 1988, organises a number of festivals and presents his own country music show on national radio. Stakėnas fills his songs with whatever takes his fancy, from the eccentric and burlesque to the occasional tearful ballad or more traditional Country & Western songs, and cites such diverse inspirations as the Soviet Russian underground figure Artiom Troitsky, Bob Dylan, and a young band from Iceland called The Sugarcubes, who played in Vilnius in 1989 fronted by a then unknown singer called Björk.

The Lithuanian Country Music Association was founded in 1995 by the outstanding violinist and Lithuanian folklore expert Algirdas Klova. Klova (1958–), a graduate of the prestigious Vilnius Conservatory (now the Vilnius Music and Theatre Academy) dabbles in everything from folk to country to bluegrass and is well worth investigation.

Of the scores of country music events taking place all over Lithuania each year, the Visagino Country international country music festival (*see p27*), one of the biggest international country music festivals in Eastern Europe, takes place in the Soviet city of Visaginas (*see p125*) and is one of the strangest and most enjoyable events of the country's cultural calendar.
Lithuanian Country Music Association. www.zona.lt/country
Virgis Stakėnas. www.stakenas.ot.lt

Children

While there aren't too many attractions specifically designed for children in Lithuania, they will not be short of things to do. The Baltic coast offers all the usual beach-related activities and water sports. The national parks are crammed with things for children to do from boating and walking to visiting folk museums and outdoor playgrounds. There are plenty of child-friendly facilities throughout the country as well, including designated play areas at beaches, parks, cities and service stations. You'll also find crèches and play areas in most shopping malls.

It's worth noting that journeys around the country by public transport can be lengthy, so if you are taking a long-distance train or bus, remember to take along plenty of books, games, snacks and drinks. Also bear in mind that many long-distance buses in Lithuania still do not operate on-board toilet facilities. Many but not all buses on long journeys make scheduled stops of ten minutes or so in towns along the way. If in doubt, ask your hotel or somebody at a tourist information centre to find out. None of the major bus companies or

Children enjoying themselves in a boat

the national railway company provide any information services in English *(see p187)*.

Children are welcome in most hotels, restaurants and cafés. Hotels offer good value on family rooms, and some of the large, modern hotels have child-minding facilities as well as rooms with sofa-beds for children. Restaurants often offer children's menus or will provide half portions on request, although finding things such as child-size cutlery and crockery or more than one high chair remains pretty much a fruitless task in almost all restaurants in the country. Some provide play areas for children. There are also a number of specifically child-oriented places to eat and to be entertained.

Beaches

Palanga (*see pp94–7*) is the number-one fun beach resort on Lithuania's Baltic coast, offering a wide, sandy beach, good swimming and plenty of snacks and ice cream for sale. There are water sports, pedaloes and a whole host of other amusements for children available on and around the beach here, plus a multitude of non-beachy things for the little ones to do, including fairground rides along Palanga's main street, Basanavičiaus. The Curonian Spit (*see pp100–107*) has a long dune-fringed beach on its western shore, and the eastern side faces the Curonian Lagoon, with water sports, including canoeing and sailing, on offer. Bicycle and rollerblade hire are available in all holiday resorts, including many places inside the country's national parks. The small beach resort of Šventoji north of Palanga and close to the Latvian border is a popular place for parents to take their children for a more relaxed break, although the resort remains very much a Lithuanian affair.

Cycling

The flatness of the land makes cycling a perfect pastime for the whole family. For information on hiring bikes, cycle maps, tours, repairs and anything else you need to know about bikes, log on to the excellent *www.bicycle.lt*. Most major towns and cities now have cycle lanes, although be warned that motorists still regard people on bicycles as fair game. Cycling in parks is an increasingly popular pastime among the locals and can offer an interesting diversion for a couple of hours.

Water sports

A huge variety of water sports are available for children countrywide. These include seaside water sports such as swimming, surfing and sailing and, in the national parks, there are many other water-based sports such as rowing, canoeing and swimming. Ask in the local tourist information centres for details of what's on offer. There are now huge indoor water parks in both Vilnius and Druskininkai (*see below*) providing year-round adventures for adults and

children alike.
Druskininkų Aqua Park. Vilniaus 13. Tel: (8-313) 52 338.
Vilnius Vichy Aquapark. Ozo 14c. Tel: (8-5) 211 11 12.

Winter activities

In winter, there are many opportunities around the country for ice-skating and sledging. Ask at local tourist information centres for details of what is available in the area. Any of the tourist information centres listed in this guide can provide more information on winter sports in their area.

The following listings cover the main attractions for children in Vilnius, Kaunas and Klaipėda.

VILNIUS

Child-friendly cafés

Išdykėlių Sala
Naugarduko 97. Tel. (8-5) 213 58 41.
Nykštukų Pasaulis
Laisvės 88. Tel: (8-5) 240 70 70.

Cinemas

Vilnius' main multiplex cinemas show the latest Hollywood films and others in their original languages with Lithuanian subtitles.

Coca Cola Plaza
Savanorių 7. Tel: 15 67.
Forum Cinemas Akropolis
Akropolis, Ozo 25. Tel: 15 67.
Skalvija
Goštauto 2/15. Tel: (8-5) 261 05 05.

Indoor playgrounds

Europa
Konstitucijos 7a.
Mauglis
Žirmūnų 1e.

Museum

Lietuvos Geležinkelių Muziejus (Lithuanian Railway Museum)
A quaint little museum covering the history of the railway in Lithuania. Children will particularly like the large train set on display.
Mindaugo 15. Tel: (8-5) 269 37 41.

Sport and leisure

Ice Palace (Ledo Rūmai)
Ažuolyno 9. Tel: (8-5) 242 44 44.

Theatres and puppet shows

Elfų Teatras
Konstitucijos 23b. Tel: (8-5) 272 60 52.
Keistuolių Teatras
Laisvės 60. Tel: (8-5) 242 45 85.
Lėlė Puppet Theatre
Arklių 5. Tel: (8-5) 262 86 78.
Raganiukės Teatras
Stanevičiaus 24. Tel: (8-670) 97 832.

KAUNAS

Cinemas

Forum Cinemas
Akropolis, Karaliaus Mindaugo 49. Tel: 15 67.

Museums

Museum of Children's Literature
Donelaičio 13. Tel: (8-37) 20 64 88.

Sport and leisure

Children and Students' Leisure Palace
Parodos 26. Tel: (8-37) 42 32 05.
Kaunas Swimming School Vilija
Demokratų 34a. Tel: (8-37) 42 34 92.
Ledo Arena Ice Skating
Aušros 42c. Tel: (8-37) 33 06 20.

Notas Tennis Courts
Veiverių Plentas 151.
Tel: (8-676) 22 901.
Tennis Court
Sporto 3.
Tel: (8-682) 23 450.
Yachting and Diving Centre
Pramonės 15.
Tel: (8-37) 76 43 90.

Theatres

Puppet Theatre
Next door to the puppet theatre is a small restaurant designed for children. There is a variety of large colourful toys for kids to play with, too.
Laisvės 87a.
Tel: (8-37) 22 00 63.
Vilkolakis Children's and Youth Theatre
Kovo 11-osios 108.
Tel: (8-37) 31 37 12.

Zoo

Lietuvos Zoologijos Sodas (Kaunas Zoo)
Not a magnificent zoo but the only one in the country. It contains over 250 different species.
Radvilėnų 21.
Tel: (8-37) 33 25 40.

KLAIPĖDA

Cinemas

Jūratė ir Kastytis
Taikos 105.
Tel: (8-46) 34 28 57.

Sport and leisure

Gintaras Swimming Pool
Daukanto 29.
Tel: (8-46) 41 09 68.
Klaipėda Sports Centre
Daukanto 24.
Tel: (8-46) 40 17 36.

A waterpark at Druskininkai

Sport and leisure

Lithuania is blessed with large areas of outstanding natural beauty and this is reflected in the local population's enthusiastic participation in outdoor sports and activities. As a consequence, there are many kilometres of designated trails for cycling and hiking. Lithuanian tourism is still relatively undeveloped, so the visitor might find that detailed information on areas outside the main cities is hard to come by, at least in English. However, with a little perseverance you can enjoy some stunning landscapes in relative tranquillity.

Lithuania's many and varied national parks and countryside provide the perfect setting for horse riding, fishing and other activities. Lithuania is also a nation with strong traditions in team sports, with basketball in particular verging on a national religion. In addition to these land-based activities, Lithuania boasts many facilities for rowing, canoeing and sailing on its numerous lakes. For the less adventurous, hiring motorised boats is a popular and relatively affordable option.

Basketball

Of the three Baltic States, Lithuania is best known as a sporting nation, mainly based on the strength and popularity of its national basketball league, which consistently draws the largest and loudest crowds of all the spectator sports.

Lithuania's association with basketball began in 1920, when national aviation hero Steponas Darius (*see p84*) returned to the country after a period living in the USA. Darius was responsible for introducing many sports to Lithuania but it was basketball that really caught the local imagination. In 1922 he established the national basketball league and the game has gone from strength to strength ever since. **Žalgiris Kaunas** is the dominant force in Lithuanian basketball and the team have won the European championship several times. Their arch rivals are the Vilnius team, **Lietuvos Rytas**. When the two teams play together every television set in the country is tuned in to the game. Tickets for live events are snapped up fast, and for the Western pocket are extremely cheap. The **Lithuanian Basketball Federation** organises the national league and provides details of teams and fixtures.

Lithuanian Basketball Federation. Birželio 23-osios 5, Vilnius. Tel: (8-5) 233 83 38. www.krepsiniofederacija.lt

Lietuvos Rytas. Siemens Arena, Ozo 14, Vilnius. http://bc.lrytas.lt
Žalgiris Kaunas. Perkūno 5, Kaunas. www.zalgiris.lt

Cycling

In many ways the Lithuanian countryside is perfectly suited to exploration by bicycle. Its undemanding terrain, low levels of traffic, extensive network of surfaced roads and ever-changing landscape makes cycling a joy. Various companies offer organised cycling tours and this is an increasingly popular option for many travellers. However, with a little research, independent bicycle trips are relatively easy to organise. Many cyclists pass through Lithuania as part of a wider tour of the Baltic States. The best known route is the Baltic Coast Cycle Route (EuroVelo route 10 from Būtingė to Nida), covering the whole length of Lithuania's Baltic coastline. There are also cycle routes in the Žemaitija National Park, Kurtuvònai, the Nemunas Loop and Panemunės Regional Park. Cycle hire, repair and cycling supplies are readily available in many towns and the non-profit organisation **Du Ratai** ('Two Wheels', *www.dvratis.lt*) will even let you hire a bicycle in Lithuania and return it in Estonia or Latvia. Everything you needed to know about cycling in Lithuania and the Baltics can be found at the superb *www.bicycle.lt*

Fishing

Lithuania offers excellent opportunities for a wide range of fishing, and this is a great way to enjoy the country's unspoilt lakes and rivers. Coarse fishing

Cycling is a pleasure along the coast in Nida

(for carp, tench, bream and the like) is popular, and Lithuania is also home to some of Europe's best pike fishing. Fly-fishing for trout and grayling is also good, and numerous companies offer fully inclusive fly-fishing holidays. The fishing season runs from April to November, although it should be noted that there are restrictions on fishing for certain species within this period. Hardy anglers can try ice-fishing in the winter months on Lithuania's numerous frozen lakes. Vodka is traditionally consumed in liberal quantities to keep the cold at bay. **Active Holidays** (*www.activeholidays.lt*) offer organised ice-fishing trips that include all the necessary safety equipment and permits.

Lake Galve in Trakai National Park is a pleasant spot for a walk

Note that to fish in public waters in Lithuania you must obtain a fishing permit. Permits can be purchased from fishing shops and fishing clubs and these are also great places to get advice on local conditions. Salmon and trout can only be fished in specific regions and a special licence is required.

Hiking

Lithuania is ideal for hiking; a quarter of the land area is forested and there are five national parks and many other conservation areas and regional parks of outstanding natural beauty. There are kilometres of hiking trails in all of these parks and the wider countryside. One of the highlights is the Aukštaitija National Park, a vast area of pine forests and lakes, interspersed with something like 100 historic Lithuanian villages. The Curonian Spit National Park is another favourite. There are walks along the unique landscape of the spit including areas of large sand dunes and several pine forests. The spit is also an excellent location for mushrooming. Trakai National Park provides the perfect location for a day trip from Vilnius.

Soccer

Lithuania doesn't have a strong football (*futbolas*) tradition, but this is rapidly changing as the sport grows in popularity. International matches are played at Kaunas' **Dariaus ir Girėno Stadionas**.

Dariaus ir Girėno Stadionas. Perkūno 5, Kaunas. www.sportohale.lt
Lietuvos Futbolo Federacija (Lithuanian Football Association). Šeimyniškių 15, Vilnius. Tel: (8-5) 263 87 41. www.futbolas.lt

Vilnius health clubs and gyms

Body Gym
Holds aerobic sessions with qualified local instructors.
Olimpiečių 3. Tel: (8-5) 272 77 44.

Forum Sports Club
Gym, pool, saunas, aerobics, massage, solarium, etc.
Konstitucijos 26. Tel: (8-5) 210 31 23.

Grožio Terapijos ir Kosmetologijos Centras
A modern and professional beauty studio that offers a host of skin and body treatments. They also hold a range of aerobics classes and have a pool complex with saunas and Jacuzzis. The centre features a large workout room and hotel.
Sugiharos 3. Tel: (8-5) 270 57 10.

AND NOW FOR SOMETHING A LITTLE DIFFERENT...

Vilniaus Aeroklubas
Offers parachute jumps from Russian aircraft at various altitudes. Beginners must take a compulsory three-hour training course.
Kyviskeš village, Vilnius. Tel: (8-5) 232 57 18.

Žiemos Sporto Centras (Winter Sports Centre)
Cross-country skiing trails in winter and a good ski jump. The trails are great for biking, hiking and running in the summer.
Sporto 3, Ignalina. Tel: (8-29) 54 193.

Food and drink

Lithuania offers a wide range of delicious natural foods. Traditional dishes are usually prepared according to season and with what nature provides. In many restaurants you'll find traditional dishes and, in most, a range of internationally recognised cuisine as well. Many places offer a wide range of game dishes, prepared according to age-old recipes. Whilst within the country's borders it's essential that you try at least one classic dish. If you can't stomach a plate of pigs' ears with your beer then at least have a go at some cepelinai.

WHAT TO EAT

Appetisers

In most pubs and restaurants the appetiser menus vary depending upon what you are drinking. For example, there are different cheese plates on offer to accompany beer (*prie alaus*) and to go with wine. Bar food that accompanies beer includes smoked or boiled pigs' ears and fried bread with an abundance of raw crushed garlic and/or cheese (*kepta duona*). Other entrées may include boiled tongue, vegetables in crispy beer batter or smoked fish. Most of these dishes are eaten with fried crackling bacon and sour cream.

International cuisine

For those of you who would rather stick to what you know, don't panic; there's a wide range of international restaurants to choose from, especially in Vilnius and the country's larger towns and cities, including Chinese (which serve truly traditional Chinese food unlike much of the Chinese food served in restaurants in the UK), Japanese, Hungarian, French, Italian, Spanish, Scandinavian and, in Vilnius only, Indian (*see p167*). Most traditional restaurants also offer a range of international dishes, and almost every restaurant in the country serves pizza, which is rapidly becoming the national dish and should be covered in a thick layer of tomato ketchup for the classic Lithuanian pizza experience. Seafood dishes, which on the whole are extremely good, are available in a few restaurants, especially, as you'd expect, along the coast. Fixed-price meals (*kompleksiniai*) are available in many restaurants and cafés during the afternoon, with many places now calling them 'business lunches' and charging extra for the more Westernised moniker.

Traditional dishes

Each region of Lithuania prepares different local dishes, depending on the produce available in that area and its historical and ethnic background. However, in almost every restaurant in the country you will find traditional dishes. Cold beetroot soup (*šaltibarščiai*) is served during the summer with a side dish of hot boiled potatoes, and is probably the best-known (and best-loved) traditional dish in Lithuania after the mighty *cepelinai* (*see box p162*). *Šaltibarščiai* is made from grated raw beetroot, sour cream (*kefiras*) with chopped cucumber, and sliced boiled eggs added for colour and flavour.

Pork (*kiauliena*) is the most popular meat and almost every part of the animal is consumed. The ears and trotters are very popular appetisers, along with pork fillets in breadcrumbs (*karbonadas*), and feature on all but the most exclusive menus.

The proximity of the Baltic Sea and the Curonian Lagoon means that fish is plentiful in Lithuania and is served in most restaurants. On the Curonian Spit you'll find roadside stalls selling a variety of smoked fish (*see pp106–7*).

Another popular traditional dish is *lietiniai*, sometimes also referred to as *blyneliai*. These are pancakes and are made with various sweet and savoury fillings, almost identical to Russian *blyni*, but renamed for essentially patriotic reasons.

Seafood dishes are particularly good

A classic dish found in many restaurants is *naminės salotos*, a traditional Lithuanian salad made of boiled potatoes, carrots and peas mixed together with mayonnaise into a sort of gloop.

Vegetarian food

The idea of vegetarian food (*vegetariškas maistas*) is a concept Lithuanians still fail to grasp. Vilnius' sole vegetarian restaurant, Balti Drambliai (*see p166*) provides a welcome respite for desperate herbivores, but even in the average eatery, there are always plenty of salads and potato-based dishes to keep strict vegetarians from starving to death. As in much of Continental Europe, vegetarians are considered an amusing oddity in Lithuania.

Restaurant/bar sign in Vilnius

CEPELINAI

Although relatively new, dating from World War I, Lithuania's mighty *cepelinai* (zeppelins) are considered the nation's national dish. Peculiar cuisine indeed, *cepelinai* are made from a mixture of mashed and finely grated raw potato formed into the shape of an airship, filled with minced meat or in some cases cottage cheese (*varškė*), and boiled for around 45 minutes. The resulting steaming lumps are then either covered in sour cream (*grietinė*) or a heart-stopping portion of fried pork fat and onions (*spirgučiai*), eaten in industrial quantities and washed down with lashings of cold beer and vodka. An interesting variation on the *cepelinai* theme is deep-fried *cepelinai*, which can be sampled in Vilnius' Čili Kaimas restaurant (*see p166*). As one would expect, home-made *cepelinai* are the best, but if you are not able to sample these, the ones served in Vilnius' Forto Dvaras restaurant (*see p167*) are generally considered to be the best.

Desserts and cakes

Lithuanian desserts aren't particularly creative. Mixed fruit, ice cream and pastries are the most common as well as the most popular choices available. With the advent of the swanky high street café in the main cities, however, the pastry and cake business is thriving, and sugar junkees will be happy to discover that they're never short of a place to satisfy their cravings.

WHAT TO DRINK

Beer

Almost without exception, Lithuanian beer (*alus*) is light, crisp, cold, cheap and delicious. Many varieties exist and you are recommended to test a few before settling on a regular brand. *Alus* tastes infinitely better from a bottle than from a tap, especially as many barmen in Lithuania aren't very good at keeping their pipes clean. Among the more common varieties are the delicious Utenos (go for the one with the blue label if you can) and Švyturys Extra. The latter comes from Klaipėda and is technically German, but that shouldn't stop anyone from drinking it. Lithuania porter (*porteris*) is also available in most bars and is fairly decent. Expect to pay anything from 4Lt to 15Lt for half a litre depending on whether you're drinking in a small local bar or a 4-star hotel.

POTATOES

The humble potato (*bulvė*) is the primary source of food in Lithuania and provides the average Lithuanian with their staple diet. There are a number of national dishes that use the potato as their main constituent, the most famous being *cepelinai* (*see box opposite*). *Bulviniai blynai* (literally, potato pancakes) is a popular dish made from raw potato, passed through a very fine grater, combined with egg and then blanched in scorching hot oil. Sometimes served with meat inside and usually with lashings of sour cream on top, potato pancakes really are a must for any visitor to Lithuania who doesn't have a heart problem. Another popular potato-based vegetarian dish is *kugelis*. From the Yiddish *kugel*, they come in the shape of a small slab, and are made, quite simply, of mashed potato cooked in the oven.

Coffee and tea

Coffee (*kava*) is found all across Lithuania. It's drunk in a number of ways including *paprasta* (boiling water poured straight on top of coffee grounds) and from a packet. Some of the better cafés, restaurants and hotels in the country have learnt the art of making good espresso. Tea (*arbata*) is drunk without milk and almost always with sugar. Some people like to stir in a spoonful of jam, something that tastes better than it sounds. Think sweet fruit tea.

Vegetarians will need to be resourceful ...

A riverside eatery in Vilnius

Spirits

Among the many locally produced spirits, two of particular note are vodka and starka. Like most Eastern Europeans, the Lithuanians are fond of vodka (*degtinė*), often to excess. Of the many fine brands two to watch out for are *Sobieski* and *Gera*. Drink 100g shots ice cold, and down in one. Lithuanian vodka is generally better and far cheaper than a certain Scandinavian import. Starka, which probably gets its name from the joining of the two Slavic words *stari* (old) and *vodka*, has been around since the 15th century and is a joint Lithuanian-Polish creation, about the only thing the two countries can agree on. A dark, almost syrupy vodka made from rye grain and flavoured with apple leaves and lime flowers, starka was traditionally buried in oak barrels on the day a daughter was born, then dug up and drunk on the day she married. For those who can't wait that long, it's now widely available in bars and restaurants. Nobody makes a bad starka. All brands are highly recommended.

Wine

For a country that spends a considerable amount of time every year under a thick blanket of snow, it is hardly surprising that Lithuania is not known as one of the great wine-growing regions of the world. Having said that, Lithuanian wines do exist, notably in the form of traditional fruit and berry wines, especially from the Aukštaitija region. The Anykščių Vynas factory (*see pp126–7*) produces a range of them, of which many are exceptionally good. You will find bottles for sale in a number of supermarkets throughout the country.

SERVICE

Good old-fashioned Western service is still a long way off in all but the most exclusive restaurants in Lithuania, partly due to the country's Soviet heritage and partly due to the fact that eating out remains primarily a necessity rather than an event in itself in the country. Getting what you want in what you would consider to be a reasonable amount of time is still a gamble. Tipping is on the increase, being still almost exclusively something that foreigners do. If you do feel the waiting staff deserve a little something for their efforts, 10 per cent is considered fair recompense. Be careful not to thank your waiter or waitress as you pay the bill as this is considered an invitation to pocket all the change, a situation that can be embarrassingly difficult to get out of.

WHERE TO EAT

With very few exceptions, eating out remains a laughably cheap and, if you choose carefully, thoroughly enjoyable experience in Lithuania. Service can be a little slow and you might not always get what you asked for, but if you don't mind being served by an army of free-thinkers in short skirts you're bound to have a wonderful time. The price ratings below indicate the price of a meal per person, without drinks.

★ under 20Lt
★★ 20–40Lt
★★★ 40–60Lt
★★★★ over 60Lt

Waiting staff in traditional costume

A restaurant in Šventoji near Palanga

Vilnius

Balti Drambliai ★

The only vegetarian restaurant in town also features a nice outdoor summer terrace with occasional (loud) live music. The food is simple, as indeed is often the case with the service, and the portions are usually enormous.

Vilniaus 41.

Tel: (8-5) 262 08 75.

Open: Mon–Fri 11am–midnight, Sat & Sun noon–midnight.

Čili Kaimas ★★

Live chickens and waitresses in traditional costumes await customers in a restaurant that combines traditional food and décor with some of the most modern service in the country. Excellent value, quality food in the heart of the old town.

Vokiečių 8.

Tel: (8-5) 231 25 36.

Open: Sun–Thur

10am–midnight, Fri & Sat 10am–2am.

Dubliner ★★
As the name suggests, the menu here is Irish, of which the limited dishes on offer are all excellent. There's also a range of international dishes, the best English-style chips in the country and a friendly atmosphere.
Dominikonų 6.
Tel: (8-5) 243 08 05.
Open: Sun–Thur 11am–midnight, Fri & Sat 11am–2am.

Forto Dvaras ★★
Another traditional Lithuanian restaurant, this one with wonderful outdoor summer seating on one of the city's oldest and most popular streets. Among the many dishes, the *cepelinai* here are considered the best available at any restaurant in the country.
Pilies 16.
Tel: (8-5) 261 10 70.
Open: 11am–midnight.

Sue's Indian Raja ★★★
Authentic and generally superb Indian food cooked by hand-picked Indian chefs in pleasant surroundings opposite the cathedral. Run by a gregarious former Indian Air Force pilot, the restaurant has dishes that are often named after customers who come to eat them on a regular basis.
Odminių 3.
Tel: (8-5) 266 18 88.
Open: 11am–midnight.

Tores ★★★
The mediocre international fare and average service on offer in this classy Užupis eatery pale into insignificance thanks to the astonishingly beautiful view of the old town at the bottom of the hill. Reserving a table on or in the terrace is highly recommended.
Užupio 40.
Tel: (8-5) 262 93 09.
Open: 11am–midnight.

Stikliai ★★★★
Arguably the best restaurant in Vilnius inside the best hotel in Vilnius, here you'll find sumptuous surroundings, impeccable service and a menu of outstanding international dishes and complementary wines.
Stikliai Hotel, Gaono 7.
Tel: (8-5) 264 95 80.
Open: Mon–Fri noon–3pm & 6pm–midnight, Sat & Sun noon–midnight.

Kaunas

Bernelių Užeiga ★★
Translating more or less as Bernie Inn, once you're over the joke (it doesn't appear to be intentional) you're left with a classic Lithuanian restaurant with all the trimmings, and portions to leave you bursting.
Valančiaus 9.
Tel: (8-37) 20 09 13.
Open: Sun–Thur 11am–midnight, Fri & Sat 11am–1am.

Medžiotojų Užeiga ★★★
A classic white-tablecloth affair with a hunting theme twist, this is a great place for carnivores to tuck into dishes of superb wild boar, beaver and other unusual surprises, all the while surrounded by stuffed animals of every shape and size. There are good set business lunches too.
Rotušės Aikštė 10.
Tel: (8-37) 32 09 56.
Open: 11am–midnight.

Klaipėda

With the exception of Kalifornija, the other Klaipėda nightclubs (*see 'Nightlife' listings, pp150–51*) serve international and local food of excellent quality, thus doubling as fine restaurants.

Delano ★

A self-service extravaganza providing hot and cold nourishment from Lithuania and beyond, the food is generally excellent and really good value to boot. The setting amidst a fairytale world complete with a huge mechanical clock is especially fun for kids, but also of interest to anyone with even a slight appreciation for the absurd.

Akropolis, Taikos 61.
Tel: (8-46) 46 91 36.
Open: 8am–midnight.

Nida

Ešerinė ★★

With a marvellous lagoon-side location for what on first sight appears to be the film set from a remake of *South Pacific*, this fabulous find at the very southern tip of Nida churns out adequate fare including both local and international dishes. Worth a visit for the truly wonderful setting.

Naglių 2.
Tel: (8-469) 52 757.
Open: 10am–midnight.

An open-air restaurant in Palanga

Palanga

During the height of the season Palanga's multitude of restaurants fill to bursting, so that, unless you want to go hungry, you just have to learn to put up with the sometimes lengthy waiting times. Eating in Palanga is more about looking cool on a terrace than what you put inside your mouth. Most restaurants are only open during the summer, and guessing which ones will be open next year is a tricky task indeed.

Čili Pica ★★

Inside the Šachmatinė restaurant at the seaside tip of the street, Čili Pica focus their attention on serving a dazzling array of decent pizzas as well as a few pasta and meat dishes for a good price, usually at high speed, and by a bevy of beautiful waitresses.

Basanavičiaus 45.
Tel: (8-460) 51 655.
Open: Sun–Thur

Lithuanian black bread and white cheese with honey

10am–2am, Fri & Sat 10am–4am.

Šiauliai

Zeppelini ★

Designed to resemble the inside of an airship with the use of lots of cheap, modern materials, this fun place serves up a host of meals including *cepelinai*, plus other mostly local meals based largely on fish and meat.

Neopolis, Vilniaus 47.

Tel: (8-41) 52 15 42.

Open: Mon–Fri noon–midnight, Sat & Sun noon–3am.

Trakai

Kybynlar ★

This is the best place to get traditional Karaite (*see p60*) dishes, including the famous *kibiniai* (*see p63*), from which the restaurant gets its name. Other treats include a few other pastries stuffed with meat, a number of pungent lamb dishes and meat wrapped in vine leaves.

Karaimų 29.

Tel: (8-528) 55 179.

Open: Sun & Tue–Thur 11am–10pm, Mon noon–10pm, Fri & Sat 11am–11pm.

Apvalaus Stalo Klubas ★★★

A combined international restaurant and pizza joint, this restaurant's rating as a place for fine dining is a little over-exaggerated, but the food is decent enough, and the added bonus of the breathtaking view of the castle immediately across the water makes it worth a visit.

Karaimų 53a.

Tel: (8-528) 55 595.

Open: 11am–11pm.

Hotels and accommodation

Lithuania has accommodation to suit all tastes and pockets. In the main cities there's an increasingly good choice of upmarket hotel chains, mid-range hotels, rented apartments, bed-and-breakfast accommodation, budget accommodation and hostels. In the more rural parts of the country a range of cheaper and less fancy rented apartments, hotels and bed-and-breakfast-style accommodation in local farmsteads is available. Although not always necessary, booking in advance is recommended. Accommodation is noticeably cheaper outside of the capital.

The following list of recommended hotels are price-rated based on bed and breakfast for one person sharing.

★	Budget: under 100Lt
★★	Moderate/ Standard: 100–200Lt
★★★	Expensive: 200–300Lt
★★★★	Luxury: over 300Lt

Vilnius

Comfort Vilnius ★
Perched precariously on the edge of the old town in an area that is still in the process of gentrification, this smart little hotel offers a basic accommodation experience with no trimmings beyond televisions in every room and pleasant staff. Popular with tour groups, this one books up a long time in advance during the summer.
Gėlių 5.
Tel: (8-5) 264 88 33.
www.comfort.lt

Litinterp ★
Providing quality beds in simple surroundings from the very early days of independence, Litinterp's philosophy of budget accommodation with a smile keeps packing them in year after year. An excellent location, with similar places in Lithuania's two other large cities, plus good-value car rental.
Bernardinų 7-2.
Tel: (8-5) 212 38 50.
www.litinterp.lt

Centro Kubas ★★
Set in a magnificent location, Centro Kubas is a small hotel with a countryside theme in the main lobby, with lots of old farming instruments on the walls. The rooms are simple but more than adequate. One of the best-value hotels in its category in the old town.
Stiklių 3.
Tel: (8-5) 266 08 60.
www.hotel.centrokubas.lt

Novotel ★★★
With the best rooms providing delightful views of the cathedral,

the Novotel is well worth thinking about if you're looking to splash out a bit. Expect all the treats Novotel provides worldwide plus a nice little bar that spills out onto the busy street during the summer.
Gedimino 16.
Tel: (8-5) 266 62 00.
www.novotel.com

Reval Hotel Lietuva ★★★
This Soviet-era masterpiece has received a full Norwegian makeover and is now one of the finest hotels in the city. Perched on the north bank of the Neris River, highlights include spectacular views of the city and a recommended bar on the 22nd floor (*see p147*).
Konstitucijos 20.
Tel: (8-5) 272 62 72.
www.revalhotels.com

Relais & Chateaux Stikliai ★★★★
The best hotel in Lithuania with a price tag to prove it; everything here is truly sublime. The hotel of choice for visiting dignitaries, rock stars and big-time property developers, the place offers rooms bursting with antiques, friendly and helpful staff and an equally ostentatious restaurant (*see p167*).
Gaono 7.
Tel: (8-5) 264 95 95.
www.stikliaihotel.lt

Druskininkai

Sanatorija Lietuva ★
Specialising in all manner of treatments, this central sanatorium is also open to those just looking for a hotel. A spectacular blast-from-the-past experience, the rooms aren't going to win any design awards, but this kind of experience is something that's bound to cease forever some time soon. A truly unique and fun experience.

The entrance of the Relais & Chateaux Stikliai

Metropolis hotel in Kaunas

Kudirkos 45.
Tel: (8-313) 52 833.
www.sanatorijalietuva.lt

Europa Royale Druskininkai ★★★
Inside a beautiful 18th-century mansion in the heart of the town, the Europa Royale Druskininkai is just as good as it sounds. Part of a chain of hotels that prides itself on its style and excellent customer service, this is the place to head for the ultimate pampering experience.
Vilniaus 7.
Tel: (8-313) 42 221.
www.europaroyale.com

Kaunas

Metropolis ★★★
This once grand hotel with sweeping staircase and wide corridors ran to ruin during the Soviet period but is slowly picking itself up again. Choose from a range of rooms from bargain basement basics to pleasant renovated ones. Great location, too.
Daukanto 21.
Tel: (8-37) 20 80 81.
www.greenhillhotel.lt

Kaunas ★★★
A fine hotel indeed in an unbeatable location, the rooms are classic upmarket business class and the staff are genuinely pleased to see you. Extras worth mentioning include the above average 55° restaurant in the cellar, named after the alcohol content of one of the local drinks they serve, and a bar offering fine people-watching experiences.
Laisvės Alėja 79.
Tel: (8-37) 75 08 50.
www.kaunashotel.lt

Klaipėda

Aribė ★
An excellent-value hotel with an almost family feel to it. Rooms are light and clean and the staff go that little bit further to make your stay extra special. Its location around the corner from the local brewery adds a nice touch, and is especially good if you like your air spiced with the fresh smell of hops and yeast.
Bangų 17a.
Tel: (8-46) 49 09 40.
www.aribe.lt

Klaipėda ★★★
Another Soviet-era behemoth that's seen a complete overhaul, the Klaipėda suits the needs of all who choose to stay in it from business travellers on expense accounts to busloads of German tourists.
Naujo Sodo 1.
Tel: (8-46) 40 43 72.
www.klaipedahotel.lt

Palanga

If it's the summer and it's hot be prepared to spend time looking for a room in Palanga as hotels book up quickly. The Tourist Information Centre (*see p95*) can help find you a room in an emergency, or you can look out for the people standing around holding *kambarių nuoma* (rooms for rent) signs.

Palangos Žuvėdra ★
About as close to the beach as it gets in Palanga, close to the Botanical Park on the superbly named Avenue of Love, the basic rooms on offer come in a range of singles, doubles, triples and apartments. Billiards, table tennis and a bar are also on hand should rain interfere with your holiday plans.
Meilės 11.
Tel: (8-460) 53 253.
www.palangos-zuvedra.lt

Šachmatinė ★★
Small but with a wide range of rooms for its size, plus a luxury apartment barely a towel's length from the sea, this strange-looking, glass-fronted hotel comes with its own club in the basement plus bicycle rent and even a small business centre.
Basanavičiaus 45.
Tel: (8-460) 51 655.
www.sachmatine.lt

Panevėžys

Panevėžys ★
Close to the bus station and overlooking the city's main pedestrianised street, the Panevėžys has come a long way since its grand Soviet beginnings. Whilst there remain a few unrenovated rooms on offer, much of the hotel has now been brought up to a fairly decent standard.
Laisvės Aikštė 26.
Tel: (8-45) 50 16 01.
www.hotelpanevezys.lt

Šiauliai

Šiauliai ★
This tall building dominating the city centre provides excellent-value accommodation in basic rooms with the added bonus of a fascinating view of the city if you ask for a room at the top. Extras include an in-house hairdresser and the cheesy Martini Club.
Draugystės 25.
Tel: (8-41) 43 73 33.
www.hotelsiauliai.lt

Visaginas

Aukštaitija ★
Apart from the extraordinary Visagino Country festival (*see p27*), the only reason to visit Visaginas would be to soak up its Soviet pedigree. Although a number of renovated rooms are available, the original rooms, still complete with plastic radios on the wall, are the real reason to spend a night here.
Veteranų 9.
Tel: (8-386) 74 858.

Practical guide

Arriving

Arriving in Lithuania has become relatively trouble-free, especially by air. If you're travelling by car, expect delays at the Russian (Kaliningrad) and Belarus borders. The delays that used to be experienced at the Latvian and Polish borders have all but vanished with all three countries now being EU members.

Visa and entry formalities

Visitors from the EU, USA, Canada, Australia, New Zealand, Switzerland and all Nordic countries can enter Lithuania without a visa for up to 90 days within a 12-month period. UK and Republic of Ireland passport holders can stay for up to twice this long within the same period. Visas aren't issued at the border and must be obtained in advance from your nearest Lithuanian consular office. For more information see the Lithuanian Ministry of Affairs website (*www.urm.lt*).

Arriving by air

Flights change and airports constantly change as well. For up to date information on arriving at all three major Lithuanian airports, see the airport websites listed below or look at the Lithuanian pages at *www.inyourpocket.com.* Car rental (*see p180*) is available at all three airports (Vilnius, Kaunas and Palanga).

Vilnius Vilnius Airport, where most international flights arrive, is Lithuania's main and busiest airport. There are now direct flights from several major European cities including Dublin, Frankfurt, London and Paris. Although not direct, one of the popular routes is through the Nordic and Scandinavian cities. There are no direct flights to Lithuania from Australia, New Zealand or North and South America.

There are plenty of taxis available at the airport, which is only 5km (3 miles) south of the city centre. A ride will cost somewhere between 20Lt and 40Lt, considerably less if you call one in advance. Alternatively, take one of the large buses that stop in front of the arrivals hall. Bus No 1 stops outside the train station, Bus No 2 goes to Lukiškių Aikštė on Gedimino, the city's main street. Tickets cost 2.40Lt and can be bought directly from the driver.
www.vilnius-airport.lt

Kaunas Kaunas' Karmėlava airport is situated in the small village of Karmėlava, 12km (7½ miles) north of the city centre. It's a small and not very busy airport, making arriving a quick and simple procedure. The airport sees scheduled flights stopping and starting all the time, with only Ryanair providing a steady service. At the time of writing Ryanair are operating flights to the city from London Stansted, Dublin, Glasgow Prestwick, Liverpool,

Lithuania's main airport at Vilnius

Frankfurt and Shannon. Taxis wait outside the main entrance and will take you into the city for around 20Lt if you negotiate. Failure to set a price before you leave could result in a journey costing not a lot less than your flight. Alternatively, take minibus No 120 to the central bus station for 1Lt. *www.kaunasair.lt*

Palanga Tiny Palanga Airport is 25km (15 miles) north of Klaipėda and at the time of writing handles a few scheduled flights from Amsterdam, Copenhagen, Frankfurt, Hamburg, Hanover and Tallinn. There are no direct flights from the UK, although it's possible to find good-value flights via Copenhagen with SAS. Buses to Klaipėda coincide with incoming flights. A taxi can be ordered at the information desk. Expect to pay a minimum of 70Lt to get to Klaipėda by taxi. *www.palanga-airport.lt*

Arriving by bus

The advent of the low-cost airline phenomenon has more or less eradicated the need for anyone but the hardiest of long-distance bus fanatics to use this kind of transport to get to Lithuania. Unless you're coming to

Lithuania from one of the countries that surround it, there remains little point. If you are desperate to use this mode of transport, information about international bus services to Lithuania can be found online at *www.eurolines.lt*

Arriving by rail

Vilnius is directly linked by rail to Latvia, Poland, Ukraine, Belarus and Kaliningrad. No direct services run from Western Europe, and trains need to be taken via Warsaw. The route from London to Vilnius takes over 45 hours and is much more expensive than flying. The only real advantage of taking the train is if you want to stop off en route and do a bit of exploring.

Details of direct routes including timetables can be found on the Lithuanian Railways website at *www.litrail.lt*. To plan a more complicated journey, use the excellent *www.bahn.de*. Be aware that some Warsaw-Vilnius routes run through Belarus, which requires a visa.

Arriving by sea

Klaipėda, on the Baltic Sea, is Lithuania's only sea port. Ferries dock here from various locations in northern Europe. Both ferry companies listed below are in Klaipėda.

Lisco

Perkėlos 10. Tel: (8-46) 39 50 51. www.lisco.lt

Klaipėda, on the Baltic Sea, is Lithuania's only port

Scandlines

Naujoji Sodo 1. Tel: (8-46) 31 05 61. www.scandlines.lt

Timetables

For up-to-date rail and ferry timetables and routes consult the *Thomas Cook European Rail Timetable*, published monthly, available to buy online at *www.thomascookpublishing.com* or from Thomas Cook branches in the UK (*tel: 01733 41 64 77*).

Camping

Camping in Lithuania's national parks is a popular and extremely affordable way of seeing the country. However, the extreme temperatures in winter restrict camping to summer, late spring and early autumn. The Lithuanian Camping Association website is in English, has an excellent search facility, a directory of sites with GPS coordinates, and site maps.

Lietuvos Kempingų Asociacija (Lithuanian Camping Association). Slėnio 1, Trakai. www.camping.lt

Children

Children are welcome almost everywhere in Lithuania. If travelling around Lithuania by car, there are regular service stations with refreshments on the main routes, of which a few provide play areas for children. In the tourist centres, restaurants and cafés are happy to provide children's portions and many have specially designed children's menus.

Climate

Temperature is always measured in Celsius. The climate ranges between continental in the eastern part of the country and maritime towards, and on, the coast. Average annual precipitation is 66cm (26in).

Unless you're particularly keen on skiing or skating, spring, summer and autumn are the best times to visit Lithuania. The numerous national and regional parks give the visitor boundless opportunities to appreciate nature and the beauty of the changing seasons throughout the year, but winters can be extremely cold.

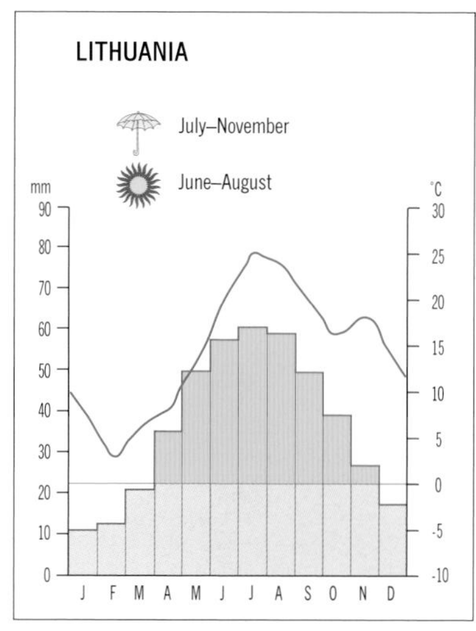

WEATHER CONVERSION CHART

25.4mm = 1 inch

°F = 1.8 × °C + 32

Crime

Lithuania is one of the safest countries in Europe, however, normal precautions are advisable. Violent crime is almost unheard of, but petty offences, notably theft, are on the increase. Be particularly vigilant in bus or train stations and in crowded locations. Exercise common sense at all times. Leaving wallets and mobile phones on tables in bars and restaurants is an open invitation.

Customs

As Lithuania is a member of the European Union there are, at least technically, no import restrictions for EU citizens. Non-EU citizens are

Be sure to complete the paperwork if you want to take an antique home

entitled to bring in 2 litres of wine, 1 litre of spirits, 200 cigarettes, 250g of tobacco and 50ml perfume. When leaving the country you can take out as much as you like tax-free, but there are tax liabilities and procedures to follow on articles over 50 years old. Enquire at the point of sale for details of the paperwork you need to complete. If in doubt, contact your local Lithuanian embassy for more information.

Driving

Driving is on the right-hand side of the road. Speed limits are generally 60kph in built-up areas and 90kph on the main roads. On two-lane highways, the speed limit is increased to 130kph from April to September and 100kph from October to March. This isn't always the rule, so keep an eye on road signs at all times. Also watch out for hidden police, as what may appear to be a rural, under-populated area may well still be in an urban speed limit area. The police are armed with speed guns and are not afraid of using them. Seatbelts are compulsory and there's a fine of 50Lt if you're caught not wearing one.

Petrol is relatively cheap by European standards, at about 3Lt–3.50Lt per litre. Petrol stations are regularly located on the main roads, some open 24 hours, but they are much less common in rural areas. The roads are generally very good on the main routes but can become quite basic in more rural areas. Ultimately, whether

CONVERSION TABLE

FROM	TO	MULTIPLY BY
Inches	Centimetres	2.54
Feet	Metres	0.3048
Yards	Metres	0.9144
Miles	Kilometres	1.6090
Acres	Hectares	0.4047
Gallons	Litres	4.5460
Ounces	Grams	28.35
Pounds	Grams	453.6
Pounds	Kilograms	0.4536
Tons	Tonnes	1.0160

To convert back, for example from centimetres to inches, divide by the number in the third column.

MEN'S SUITS

UK	36	38	40	42	44	46	48
Rest of Europe	46	48	50	52	54	56	58
USA	36	38	40	42	44	46	48

DRESS SIZES

UK	8	10	12	14	16	18
France	36	38	40	42	44	46
Italy	38	40	42	44	46	48
Rest of Europe	34	36	38	40	42	44
USA	6	8	10	12	14	16

MEN'S SHIRTS

UK	14	14.5	15	15.5	16	16.5	17
Rest of Europe	36	37	38	39/40	41	42	43
USA	14	14.5	15	15.5	16	16.5	17

MEN'S SHOES

UK	7	7.5	8.5	9.5	10.5	11
Rest of Europe	41	42	43	44	45	46
USA	8	8.5	9.5	10.5	11.5	12

WOMEN'S SHOES

UK	4.5	5	5.5	6	6.5	7
Rest of Europe	38	38	39	39	40	41
USA	6	6.5	7	7.5	8	8.5

or not you can move with ease around the country depends on the weather. Snow is a major factor here. The main roads are regularly attended to but can still be impassable in extreme conditions. Off these main roads you may have difficulty, and a four-wheel drive would be the minimum requirement to achieve any meaningful level of mobility for touring. It's better, although perhaps not as much fun, to tour in the spring, summer and autumn.

Car rental

All the main international car rental companies have offices in Lithuania. Car rental is generally expensive, with a few local exceptions. Most national and international driving licences are accepted here.

addCar
www.addCarrental.com

Avis
www.avis.lt

Budget
www.budget.lt

Europcar
www.europcar.lt

Hertz
www.hertz.lt

Rimas
A range of vehicles are available, whether you're happy with a bit of a rust bucket or would rather drive a fairly decent-looking motor. The charming people at Rimas have been providing a personal car rental service to a wide range of loyal visitors and residents since independence.
Tel. (8-6) 982 16 62.

Sixt
www.sixt.lt

Unirent
www.unirent.lt

Embassies and Consulates

The following embassies are all in Vilnius.

Australia (Consulate)
Vilniaus 23. Tel: (8-5) 212 33 69.

Canada
Jogailos 4. Tel: (8-5) 249 09 50.
www.canada.lt

Republic of Ireland
Gedimino 1. Tel: (8-5) 262 94 60.

UK
Antakalnio 2. Tel: (8-5) 246 29 00.
www.britain.lt

USA
Akmenų 6. Tel: (8-5) 266 55 00.
www.usembassy.lt

Emergency telephone numbers

Fire 01
Police 02
Ambulance 03
Gas 04
Electrical and plumbing 05

Health

Visiting Lithuania poses no great health risks although precaution is always advisable. UK and EU citizens with a valid EHIC card can receive reduced-cost or even free treatment, although private medical insurance is still worth investing in. Whereas the difference between private and public healthcare in the West is generally a question of time, state healthcare in Lithuania is of a much lower standard than its paying alternative.

Insurance

As a member of the European Union, EU healthcare privileges apply to all EU visitors but there is no harm in taking out additional personal insurance. You can obtain insurance from any travel agent or tour operator in your home country. Most insurance policies should offer adequate cover for medical expenses, theft, and loss of baggage and other personal possessions. Some policies also extend to cover travellers' cheques and even cash and personal liability. Make sure you check the exclusion clauses, extent and amount of cover. If you have home insurance cover it's worth checking it before you commit to another policy as you may well be covered for some of these eventualities already.

If you are hiring a car, the insurance package usually includes collision damage waiver (CDW) and tends to be compulsory. It's worth checking with your own motor insurance broker what your current policy covers before you leave home. Car hire firms would usually give you the option of paying a certain amount in case of an accident, but the main liability in this event will be yours. If you do have an accident in a vehicle in Lithuania, no matter how minor, don't move your vehicle, even if it's blocking all the traffic, until the police arrive on the scene. Failure to comply with this rather ridiculous and often dangerous law means you will almost certainly lose any insurance rights you have.

Take care when driving in the city

Language

The national language is Lithuanian, an Indo-European language and one of the oldest languages still spoken today. While it's close to Latvian, it has no basic similarities with the Slavic language although it has absorbed many Slavic (mostly Polish) words over the centuries. There are masculine and feminine genders in Lithuanian; masculine nouns end with the letters 'as', 'is' or 'us', and feminine nouns end with an 'a' or an 'ė'. Lithuanian is an unusual language, and it has the propensity to sound comical thanks to the necessity to change English word endings to fit its own grammatical rules (e.g. Davidas Bekhamas).

Bus timetables can be found around the post at the bus stop

Maps

Tourist information centres are a good source of both small and large maps. Each local tourist centre will have a supply of maps of the area. Most are free, and when there is a charge, it is a modest one. Petrol stations also sell maps for touring, an essential purchase if you're thinking of taking to some of the country's less-used roads. Bookshops in the main cities also stock a reasonably good supply of maps. The excellent local print and online *In Your Pocket* guide series include maps in their print publications. See *www.inyourpocket.com* for more information.

Media

Local in-depth media is in Lithuanian, Polish and Russian only. The only publication that could be called a newspaper is the pan-Baltic *Baltic Times*, published weekly and available in many hotels and bookshops. *City Paper* is the only Baltic magazine in English. A mixture of magazine-style editorial content and traditional city guides, it can also be found in many hotels. The most useful thing to read when in Lithuania are the local *In Your Pocket* guides. Available in print form to the three cities of Vilnius, Kaunas and Klaipėda, they also publish their entire content for free at *www.inyourpocket.com*. This site can prove invaluable when planning your holiday. Cable and satellite television in English is available in many hotels.

Language

This is not as complicated as you might expect. Each letter represents an individual sound and apart from a few exceptions is pronounced exactly as it looks. A few of the most difficult exceptions are as follows.

C like the ts in cats
Č like the ch in chair
Š like the sh in shoe
Y like the i in hit
Ž like the s in treasure

Numbers

1	vienas (m) viena (f)
2	du (m) dvi (f)
3	trys
4	keturi (m) keturios (f)
5	penki (m) penkios (f)
6	šeši (m) šešios (f)
7	septyni (m) septynios (f)
8	aštuoni (m) aštuonios (f)
9	devyni (m) devynios (f)
10	dešimt
20	dvidešimt
50	penkiasdešimt
100	šimtas
200	du šimtai

Useful words and phrases

Do you speak English?	ar jus kalbate angliškai?
See you!	iki!
My name is...	mano vardas…
Where is...?	Kur yra...?
Hotel	viešbutis
Street	gatvė
Hospital	ligoninė
Chemist	vaistinė
Dentist	dantų gydytojas
Bread	duona
Wine	vynas
Sugar	cukrus
Beer	alus
Coffee	kava
More please	dar prašau
Milk	pienas
Petrol	benzinas

Polite greetings

Hello	laba diena
Goodbye	viso gero
Good morning	labas rytas
Good evening	labas vakaras
Good night	labanakt
Please	prašau, prašom
Thank you	ačiū
OK	gerai

Everyday expressions

Yes	taip
No	ne
I don't understand	(aš) nesuprantu
Excuse me/sorry	atsiprašau
How much?	kiek kainuoja?
Cheap/expensive	pigūs/brangūs
Hot/cold	karštas/šaltas
Left/right	kairė/dešinė

Time

Today	šiandien
Yesterday	vakar
Tomorrow	rytoj
In the evening	vakare

Days of the week

Monday	pirmadienis
Tuesday	antradienis
Wednesday	trečiadienis
Thursday	ketvirtadienis
Friday	penktadienis
Saturday	šeštadienis
Sunday	sekmadienis

Buy a bouquet from a town centre flower shop for birthdays and feastdays

Medical services

The only hospital in Lithuania certified by all major insurance companies is the Baltic-American Clinic on the northern outskirts of Vilnius. It's a private clinic offering a wide range of Western-standard services, including family medicine and dental treatment. Gedimino Vaistinė is a good central chemist in Vilnius open around the clock. Gidenta provides excellent dental treatment for a good price, and Medicine Central Private Clinic is a recommended GP-style surgery run by an Australian doctor.

Baltic American Clinic
Nemenčinės 54a, Vilnius.
Tel: (8-5) 234 20 20. www.bak.lt

Gedimino Vaistinė
Gedimino 27, Vilnius.
Tel: (8-5) 261 01 35.

Gidenta
Vienulio 14-3, Vilnius.
Tel: (8-5) 261 71 43. www.gidenta.lt

Medicine Central Private Clinic
Gedimino 1a-19, Vilnius.
Tel: (8-5) 261 35 34. www.clinic.lt

Money matters

Currency

The unit of currency in Lithuania is the *litas* (Lt), pegged to the euro at a rate of 3.45Lt to €1. *Litas* come in note form in denominations of 10, 20, 50, 100, 200 and 500Lt. The smaller units are called *centas/centai* (ct), with 100ct making up 1Lt. The coins come in denominations of 1, 2 and 5Lt, and 1, 2, 5, 10, 20 and 50ct. An easy way to stay ahead of the game is to remember that £1 is more or less equal to 5Lt.

Credit cards and ATMs

Most upmarket restaurants, hotels, cafés and shops in main cities in Lithuania accept major credit cards, especially Visa and MasterCard. Many rural places are yet to discover the magic of plastic. Carrying a little cash at all times is highly recommended. ATM machines are in abundance in the main cities and beyond, and there are ATMs in the arrivals halls of all three major airports in the country.

Exchange

Most foreign currencies (Scottish banknotes being one of the exceptions) can be exchanged at banks and foreign exchange offices. Traveller's cheques can be changed at the bigger banks. There are also exchange kiosks in the main cities, and ATM machines can be used to withdraw local currency.

Opening hours

Work hours are not strictly regulated so those given below may vary. Work hours are sometimes shorter on Fridays and prior to public holidays.

Government institutions

Mon–Fri 8am–5pm, Sat noon–1pm.

Museums and places of interest

Many of the places listed in this guidebook operate different opening times in and out of season. The details given throughout the guide are for summer opening times. Almost all museums and places of interest don't fix their next-season opening times until near the time they actually change. Always check opening times if you're travelling a substantial distance to visit a sight.

Office hours

Mon–Fri 10am–7pm, Sat 10am–3pm.

Supermarkets

These usually operate 8am–10pm but some stay open until midnight. Some offer 24-hour services. A limited number of shops open on Sundays.

Organised tours

For locally arranged organised tours, ask at any of the tourist information centres listed in this guide. For overseas-based travel arrangements, Baltic Holidays, in the UK, is an excellent choice.

Baltic Holidays

Run by a second-generation Lithuanian and offering a galaxy of packages to Lithuania and the Baltics in general.
40 Princess Street, Manchester.
Tel: 0845 070 5711.
www.balticholidays.com

Post offices (*Paštas*)

Lithuanian post offices are recognisable by the bright yellow symbol that features the silhouette of an old postal horn. This makes them easy to spot and there are plenty of them. The post office inside Vilnius'

Akropolis (*see p142*) is open 10am–10pm seven days a week. You can buy stamps at post offices, and the service is reliable, although letters and postcards sent to the UK by air mail can easily take up to a week to arrive. *www.post.lt*

Main post offices

Vilnius

Gedimino 7. Tel: (8-5) 261 67 59.

Kaunas

Laisvės Alėja 102. Tel: (8-37) 40 13 68.

Klaipėda

Liepų 16. Tel: (8-46) 31 50 22.

Express mail

DHL

www.dhl.lt

FedEx

www.fedex.com

TNT

www.tnt.lt

UPS

www.ups.com

Public holidays

1 January New Year's Day and National Flag Day

16 February Independence Day

11 March Restoration of Independence

March/April Easter Sunday, Easter Monday

The main post office in Kaunas

1 May International Labour Day
14 June Day of Mourning and Hope
23–24 June Joninės (Feast of St John), Midsummer
6 July Day of Statehood, Crowning of King Mindaugas
15 August Žolinė (Feast of the Assumption)
23 August Black Ribbon Day (Molotov-Ribbentrop)
8 September Crowning of Vytautas the Great
25 October Constitution Day
1 November Vėlinės (All Saints Day)
24–25 December Kalėdos (Christmas)

Public transport

Long-distance buses

The most convenient, although not always the most luxurious, way of getting around the country, frequent long-distance buses operate between Lithuania's main cities as well as daily or twice-daily buses to the remoter regions. Bus stations generally have good clear departure boards, although don't expect to find anybody who speaks a word of English working at them. Unlike in the UK and most of Western Europe, buses are more expensive to use than trains in Lithuania.

Vilniaus Autobusų Stotis (Vilnius Bus Station)
Sodų 22. Tel: 16 61. www.toks.lt

Kauno Autobusų Stotis (Kaunas Bus Station)
Vytauto 24/26. Tel: (8-37) 40 90 60. www.kautra.lt

Klaipėdos Autobusų Stotis (Klaipėda Bus Station)
Butkų Juzės 9. Tel: (8-46) 41 15 47. www.klap.lt

Trains

Although cheaper than buses, services on Lithuanian Railways (Lietuvos Geležinkeliai) are not as frequent and seldom as fast as the buses; the journey from Vilnius to Klaipėda, for example, takes five hours by train, as opposed to between three or four hours on the bus. The main link between Vilnius and Kaunas has regular commuter trains, with new high-speed trains promised between the two cities from 2008. Other, longer routes are less well served. Timetables at the stations are not always available, so you're best to get your information from the website at *www.litrail.lt*

Vilniaus Geležinkelio Stotis (Vilnius Train Station)
Geležinkelio 16. Tel: (8-5) 233 00 88.

Kauno Geležinkelio Stotis (Kaunas Train Station)
Čiurlionio 16. Tel: (8-37) 27 29 55.

Klaipėdos Geležinkelio Stotis (Klaipėda Train Station)
Priestočio 1. Tel: (8-46) 29 63 85.

Words to look out for

Departures *isvyksta, isvykimo laikas, isvykimas*
Arrivals *atvyksta, atvykimo, atvykimas*
Platform *peronas*

Smoking

Smoking was banned in all restaurants, cafés and bars countrywide from 1 January 2007. It is also banned on all forms of public transport.

Sustainable tourism

Thomas Cook is a strong advocate of ethical and fairly traded tourism and believes that the travel experience should be as good for the places visited as it is for the people that visit. That's why Thomas Cook is a firm supporter of The Travel Foundation, a charity that develops solutions to help improve and protect holiday destinations, their environment, traditions and culture. To find out what you can do to make a positive difference to the places you travel to and the people who live there, please visit *www.thetravelfoundation.org.uk*

Taxis

Lithuanian taxis drivers are, on the whole, the same as taxi drivers throughout the world; if they think they can get away with overcharging foreigners, they will. There are few ways to avoid this. In general, calling in advance is cheaper than taking a taxi in the street, unless you fall prey to the overcharging described above. Official rates start at a flat fee of around 2Lt, with a kilometre rate after that of anything from 1Lt to 5Lt depending on the company you use, time of day, and where you are. On a positive note, even an expensive taxi ride in Lithuania is cheaper than one in the West, so much so that if you're travelling in a group, long-distance taxi rides are worth considering. At the time of writing, the 110km (68-mile) journey from Vilnius to Kaunas costs about 150Lt.

Telephones

Public telephones

Public telephones can be found easily in most cities and towns. You can only make calls on public phones with a call card, which can be bought from most kiosks, supermarkets and post offices. The cards come in a variety of units, ranging from 50 to 200.

Mobile telephones

At the time of writing, roaming is still fairly expensive in Lithuania, although international legislation hopefully being brought in towards the end of 2007 will put a stop to this. Alternatively, buy a local pre-paid SIM card and stick it in your phone. All three mobile operators listed provide easy-to-use, affordable pre-paid services.

Bitė
www.bite.lt

Omnitel
www.omnitel.lt

Tele 2
www.tele2.lt

Telephone codes for the main Lithuanian cities

Alytus 315
Birštonas 319

Druskininkai 313
Ignalina 386
Kaunas 37
Klaipėda 46
Lazdijai 318
Marijampolė 343
Molėtai 383
Neringa 469
Palanga 460
Panevėžys 45
Šiauliai 41
Trakai 528
Vilnius 5
Visaginas 386

Time and date

Local time is GMT + two hours. Lithuania is thus two hours ahead of the UK and the Republic of Ireland, six hours ahead of Eastern Standard Time, one hour ahead of South Africa, eight hours behind Australia and ten behind New Zealand. Clocks go forward an hour on the last Sunday of March and back again on the last Sunday of October. The form of writing dates in Lithuanian is year, month, day (2008.12.25).

Tipping

The more expensive restaurants include service on the bill, although an extra 10 per cent or at least rounding up is always appreciated, as official tips rarely make it into the hands of those they're intended for.

Toilets

There's a shortage of public toilets in Lithuania. They can be found in larger shopping centres, in petrol stations and some tourist information centres. An old habit that refuses to go away is the obsession that toilet paper won't flush away. Thus, buckets are still provided next to toilets, often even in the most expensive places. A triangle pointing up or the letter M is for ladies. A triangle pointing down or a V is for men.

Tourist information

Tourist information centres can be found in many towns and cities throughout the country, most of them providing an excellent service.

Lithuanian State Department of Tourism
Juozapavičiaus 13, Vilnius.
Tel: (8-5) 210 87 96.
www.tourism.lt

Travellers with disabilities

The lack of kerb drops and the cobblestone streets in the old towns of Lithuania's three major cities make it a bit of a bumpy ride for wheelchair users, and the public transport system countrywide needs to be completely renewed before qualifying as being even vaguely accessible. Some new 'kneeling' buses and trolleybuses are being introduced, but as yet there are very few indeed. Some hotels cater for visitors with mobility restrictions, as do a few restaurants and cafés. Sadly, many sights are completely off limits.

Index

Acknowledgements

Thomas Cook Publishing wishes to thank POLLY PHILLIMORE for the loan of the photographs reproduced in this book, to whom the copyright in the photographs belongs (except the following):

LITHUANIAN TOURIST BOARD 5, 35, 65, 67a, 75, 129, 131, 148, 168
ANDREW QUESTED 16, 18, 21, 32, 40, 41, 44, 48, 49, 61, 62, 64, 140, 141, 144, 161, 163b, 164, 165, 171
RICHARD SCHOFIELD 1, 29, 36, 45, 51, 76, 77, 92, 93, 175, 178, 181, 182
WIKIMEDIA COMMONS 58 (Juliux); 46, 85, 104 (Wojsyl); 112 (Mindaugas Urbonas); 113 (Ubiqve); 114 (Cajeton); 116 (Dezidor); 118 (Ronenakaydar); 126 (Julius); 127 (Matasg); 147 (Alma Pater); 149 (Lokyz); 150 (August BigHead); 155 (arz); 166, 168 (Thomas Pusch)
WORLD PICTURES/PHOTOSHOT 120, 157, 158
RAY VYSNIAUSKAS 172
SALANTŲ REGIONINIS PARKAS 138, 139

For CAMBRIDGE PUBLISHING MANAGEMENT LTD:
Project editor: Karen Beaulah
Typesetter: Paul Queripel
Proofreader: Penny Isaac
Indexer: Karolin Thomas

SEND YOUR THOUGHTS TO BOOKS@THOMASCOOK.COM

We're committed to providing the very best up-to-date information in our travel guides and constantly strive to make them as useful as they can be. You can help us to improve future editions by letting us have your feedback. If you've made a wonderful discovery on your travels that we don't already feature, if you'd like to inform us about recent changes to anything that we do include, or if you simply want to let us know your thoughts about this guidebook and how we can make it even better – we'd love to hear from you.

Send us ideas, discoveries and recommendations today and then look out for your valuable input in the next edition of this title.

Emails to the above address, or letters to Travellers Series Editor, Thomas Cook Publishing, PO Box 227, Unit 9, Coningsby Road, Peterborough PE3 8SB, UK.

Please don't forget to let us know which title your feedback refers to!